D1799468

As I remember

Stories from
'Sounds Historical'

volume

Compiled by Jim Sullivan

TANDEM PRESS

First published in New Zealand in 2002 by
TANDEM PRESS
2A Rugby Road
Birkenhead, Auckland
New Zealand
www.tandempress.co.nz

National Library of New Zealand Cataloguing-in-Publication Data

As I remember. Vol. 3 : stories from 'Sounds historical' / compiled by Jim Sullivan.
ISBN 1-877298-03-4
1. New Zealand—History—20th century—Anecdotes.
2. New Zealand—Social life and customs—Anecdotes. I. Sullivan, Jim, 1946–
II. Sounds historical (Radio program)
993.030922—dc 21

Cover and text design by Jacinda Torrance / Verso
Production by BookNZ
Printed in New Zealand by Publishing Press

Front cover: School Dental Nurse Urquhart with some of her patients, Te Araroa, 1942.
R.M.S. Taylor Collection, *Alexander Turnbull Library of New Zealand,*
Te Puna Matauranga o Aotearoa, F-106538-1/2.

Back cover: Thanks to Verna Morris (City Girl in the Country)
Noel Fraser (My First Car)

Introduction

The As I Remember stories on National Radio's 'Sounds Historical' continue to be a highlight for listeners as well as for myself, producer Alison Lloyd-Davies and our talented group of on-air readers.

The appeal of well-told personal stories is obviously strong and I'm sure this third collection of memories will bring much pleasure. For a taste of what might appear in Volume 4, I recommend a date with National Radio every Sunday night to hear more first-hand recollections of our past.

My thanks to all the As I Remember contributors.

Jim Sullivan
Dunedin, September 2002

Acknowledgements

Once again we must thank all the contributors for their wonderful stories and for their generosity in providing valuable photographs for publication.

Every effort was made to contact each contributor prior to publication and we apologise if we weren't able to get in touch with everyone.

Contents

Home by bus and boat in the 1930s

Alistair Kerr

WHEN I WAS a small boy in the late 1930s I used to travel to and from Christchurch and the Marlborough Sounds. My parents were managing a sheep farm on Forsyth Island at the northern end of Pelorus Sound. My two brothers were beginning their education through the Correspondence School, but it was decided that I should stay with an aunt in Christchurch for my education. For the term holidays, I went to stay on family farms in the Rangitata Gorge or at Cave in South Canterbury. However, the Christmas holidays brought the longed-for trip home and six weeks of bliss in what was a small boy's paradise – that island in the Sounds.

My journey home began very early in the morning at the Cashel Street terminus of Newman Brothers' White Star Motors. In those days the buses were known as 'service cars' and those in Newman's service were more like large cars than are the buses of today. They had seats which ran right across the body of the vehicle with a door on the left side of each row of seats. They were V8 Cadillacs and Newman's alliteratively advertised them as 'Cosy, Comfortable, Cadillac Cars'! Their drivers were dressed in a spotless white dustcoat with a white-topped nautical cap. As an unaccompanied child, I always had the place of honour on the front seat beside the driver and without exception they treated me with the utmost care and courtesy.

Most of the long trip, once we had cleared the Christchurch area, was over dusty, unsealed roads and in the height of summer it was a welcome relief when we arrived in Kaikoura for lunch. I felt most grown-up as I entered the cool, shady dining room of the hotel where there were stiff, starched tablecloths and napkins and very heavy cutlery. The menu never varied. You had a choice of roast mutton or beef with three vegetables and a steamed pudding to follow.

When we arrived in Blenheim I had to transfer to the Nelson bus, which took me the short distance to the village of Havelock at the head of Pelorus Sound. There I spent the night either with the local doctor, Dr Cantrell, or, more grandly in my opinion, in the Havelock Hotel. While I knew that the bar area was strictly off-limits, I used to sneak down by the door and absorb the smoky, beery atmosphere and feel very daring! However, it wasn't long before the tiring day I'd had and the knowledge of an early start to catch the mail-launch in the morning ensured that I was soon in my bed.

In the 1930s, the mail-launch service was run by one of the Sound's real identities, Eric Johnson, who had a launch called the *Rata*. There were no roads over the steep bush-clad hills, which divided the myriad of waterways of Pelorus Sound. There was a very unreliable telephone line so the farm families depended almost entirely on Eric's service for the regular delivery of passengers, mail and supplies. The weekly arrival of the mail-launch was an event they all looked forward to.

Next day, we made a very early start and once the narrow channel out of Havelock was cleared the journey proper began. On a fine day, the green hills reaching down to the glassy water gave some breathtaking views. Eric knew of my passion for the sea and he always allowed me to share the wheelhouse with him. At each stop we came alongside the farm wharf to land the mailbags, groceries and the occasional passenger. As we reached the outer Sound later in the morning, and the turbulent waters of Cook Strait made their presence felt, I revelled in the driven spray as the launch pounded into the head seas. I'm not sure that all the other passengers shared that pleasure!

The journey back to school at the end of the holiday was less pleasant, but I will always remember Eric's gruff kindness in insisting that, once away from the Forsyth wharf, I take the wheel while he went to the cabin to cook his lunch on the smelly Primus stove. I felt like a real old sea-dog as I made sure that I kept *Rata*'s bow well out to clear Duffers Reef before turning to starboard on the next leg to Titirangi, but I imagine Eric was keeping an eye out of the porthole, just to be sure I was going in the right direction!

There are now several roads into the area, but it's good to know that the Pelorus Sound mail-launch still provides the same good service that it did all those years ago, and that the name of Eric Johnson is still fondly remembered.

Cars on trains through the Southern Alps

Jim Dangerfield

BEFORE THE SECOND World War, I worked at the Otira railway station on the mountain divide, which separates Canterbury from the West Coast. In those days the highway was unsealed and several of the waterways unbridged. Motorcars were not always reliable in their performance and nor were their rubber tyres always efficient, so the steep gradients of Arthur's Pass were testing for both vehicles and nervous drivers. Road travel from coast to coast could be quite an unpredictable adventure, especially when shingle slips blocked the roadway. So when conditions on the highway were doubtful or the road was actually impassable, motorists called on the railways to provide transport for themselves and their vehicles between Springfield and Otira. It was irregular and unprofitable, but it supplied a much-needed service for locals and the occasional tourists – who usually wanted the train transport immediately! But train services couldn't be quickly rearranged. The regular trains couldn't be disrupted for other services on demand and it wasn't always easy to find staff and rolling stock at holiday periods to operate the motorcar specials.

The loading banks at the three stations – Springfield, Arthur's Pass and Otira – were arranged so that the motorists had only to drive forwards when loading and off-loading their vehicles. Wooden-floored

U-class bogie wagons had had their bond chains and end boards removed, and the adapted four-wheeled M-class wagons had no surrounds. Motorists who complained there were no walkways on the wagon edges were reminded that their train would pass through 17 tunnels on the way and that those tunnels imposed obvious restrictions. Portable hardwood bridges were supplied at the loading banks to make platforms between the wagons and these were adjusted to suit the vehicle being handled. There was always the nervous driver who had to be assured that the bridge and his wheels were in precise alignment for his safe crossing between wagons. There were some regular customers who ordered ahead for wagon space and had their vehicles pre-loaded ready to be attached to the regular express in which they then travelled. The casual users had to be content with travel by the slower goods trains which had three guards' vans with fitted seating for passengers.

In the 1930s travel from coast to coast certainly had its moments, especially for motorists who found that only the trains could get through.

Audrey with her brothers and other Nokomai School children in very heavy snow.

Childhood at the Nokomai Goldfields

Audrey Derrick

THE DAY SEEMED endless; the dust obliterated all we were leaving behind. The only noises were the drone of the engine and the occasional word exchanged by the adults. There were endless hills, rivers, blue sky and . . . nothing. After what seemed an eternity our truck swung to the right past a sign that said 'Glen Falloch Station' – Glen Falloch is Gaelic for 'hidden valley'. Suddenly there was life – a big homestead, shearing shed, a school and a row of six houses. We went past a paddock called Long Lion Paddock, and in my childishness I thought lions lived there, but I learned later that it was the name of the first gold-mining company.

We'd reached the end of the road. We were at the Nokomai goldfields, near Kingston at the southern end of Lake Wakatipu. In its heyday there had been 2000 people on the Nokomai goldfields but it was now the 1930s and there was just a small settlement. There were six married couples and across the creek, and around the back of the mine, were the single men's and the Chinese men's huts and living quarters. It was quite primitive. Power came from the mine generator and the wash-house was a copper set out in the open. The winters were so cold eggs froze solid if left out overnight. My mother made extra blankets from clean chaff sacks covered with cretonne material. Bricks heated in the oven and wrapped in old clothes were put on our beds at night for warmth. Baths were once a week on Saturday nights in a tin tub in front of a roaring fire in the kitchen. We cleaned our teeth with a rag dipped in salt.

Our house had a black iron range in the kitchen and a safe outside in the shade for meat and milk, which, with home-made butter, came from the Nokomai Station. My mother made her own bread – using potatoes instead of yeast. It smelled wonderful and was lovely to eat. Dad cut down beer bottles by putting a wire hoop, heated in the fire, around them then plunging them into cold water and Mum used these for jam jars, which she completely covered with newspaper using a flour and water paste. We also made ginger beer from our own starters. The bottles were corked and we were often startled by a bang as a cork blew out and hit the ceiling.

It was always a highlight of the day when the grocer came because we children were allowed to go across to the huts and tell the men he had arrived. Occasionally, an old man arrived with his horse and wagon. This was Abda Houli, a hawker. He'd lift up the canvas sides of his wagon and display his wares – materials, sheets, pots and pans – you name it, he had it.

We were a very close-knit community. The adults played euchre at night in the school and my mother usually won the booby prizes – a box of hankies or a salt and pepper set of an Indian boy and girl. During the evening the men took it in turn to walk back to the houses to check on the children.

My father usually worked night shift handling the huge hydraulic nozzle that sluiced away the hillside. The water came from around the hills in huge iron pipes and the Chinese men who tended the water race each had three miles of the race as his responsibility. They lived a lonely existence.

One day I went on a picnic with my parents and brothers. My mother slipped into the water and had to take her frock off to dry just as the mine manager came around the hill so my mother had to dive for cover in the bush as she didn't have time to put her frock back on again! The mine manager was on a horse – the first I'd ever seen. It was a roan colour and had a jingling harness; it made a snorting noise as it ate the grass.

The early miners had planted gooseberry bushes, wild briar roses and plum trees, and one day the mothers and children were gathering wild gooseberries from the hills at the back of the school when someone spied a car stopping at the front. It was the church minister. At once the women smoothed their hair and took off their aprons. They left their baskets on the porch and sat down at the desks. I don't know what was said but it was all very solemn and every woman listened intently. That was the first time I'd seen a minister preach.

When I was seven, in 1933, we left Nokomai because my mother was expecting another baby and it was too isolated for her to stay there. I went back two or three times later; once when I was 13, for a holiday before I started work.

Now I never go to Queenstown without looking in towards the hills at Parawa. The sign says Nokomai Station but to me it will always be Glen Falloch, the hidden valley, where I spent part of my childhood.

City girl in the country

Verna Morris

I WAS A schoolgirl when I first visited Central Otago to stay on my uncle's farm at Teviot near Roxburgh. We visited neighbours three or four miles further on at Kirribilli. It had been part of the old Teviot Run, which was subdivided into rehab farms for returned servicemen after the First World War.

Ten years after my schoolgirl visit I was teaching at Ettrick school across the Clutha River from Teviot. I met Frank Morris at a local Plunket ball, there was an instant rapport, and six months later we were married. From city girl to a 1950s backblocks pioneer was quite a learning experience. I settled on that farm I had visited as a child, Kirribilli. It was over 4000 acres of tussock country carrying sheep and cattle with some cultivation for winter feed. The farmhouse was above the snow line, about 1600 feet above sea level. This is an area with extremely heavy frosts and when I boarded with a family before I was married I had a bedroom on the cold side of the house. On frosty nights I wore pyjamas, a pullover, socks, gloves, a hat, another jersey wrapped around my rump, and I had a hot-water bottle! When I woke in the morning the sheet would be frozen stiff where I'd breathed on it in the night.

When I got married, our first house was built of huts put together but it was sunny and comfortable. There was no electricity at first, so at night we used kerosene lamps and candles. The wash-house was a lean-to outside the back door with a copper and tubs. On frosty winter mornings the washing would freeze on the line before I put in the second peg. The eggs in the fowl-house even froze in the nests and their shells cracked. The house was heated by the coal range, open fire, and an early-model, closed-door burner. The water was heated by the coal range and we would bank up the fire before going to bed so we could have plenty of hot water in the morning. Coal was plentiful. It came from a coal-mine near Roxburgh and was fairly dull but it was cheap and we could get it by the truckload. Some of our wood came from pine trees on the farm, and the rest was bought locally.

I loved life on the farm though I wasn't the best cook and had to cope with the old Shacklock coal range. My days were filled with food and then babies as well. Shopping was usually done only once a week, sometimes fortnightly when the mail was collected at the foot of the hill, so we got used to eating stale bread.

After my first effort at cutting hair, Frank drove 11 miles to the barber in Roxburgh for some repair work. However, he didn't give up on me and for the next 45 years I was the family hairdresser.

There was great excitement when Frank bought a second-hand power generator. It ran only the lights and was supposed to be controlled by a button indoors, but this system failed many times and after reading in bed Frank would often have to get up and go to the shed outside to turn the power off for the night. The arrival of electric power made life much easier. It greatly improved our knowledge of what was happening in the world outside as we could then have a radio.

The phone was a party line, which closed at midnight from

Monday to Saturday and at eight o'clock on Sunday nights. If the phone line was knocked down by a storm or by cattle, Frank had to walk about three miles across steep country to find and fix the fault. If he found the fault but couldn't fix it then he had to contact the authorities.

Another pleasing development was the installation of the septic tank. It was a great novelty to pull a chain instead of having a long-drop toilet, but we had to be careful about our use of water. It came from an underground creek uphill from the house, was fed into the tank and then gravitated to the house while another tank caught rainwater from the roof.

Frank made a lake on the farm and bought an old fire engine to use for irrigation. A top-dressing pilot flew over the area one day and nearly crashed when he suddenly spotted a fire engine in the middle of a lake, in the middle of nowhere.

A Christmas jewel

Belle Robertson Avery

IN 1934 MY Scottish parents were dairy farmers in the Bay of Plenty. We lived on Onepu Road, which approached the foothills of Mount Edgcumbe and we also had a distant view of Mount Tarawera. I was 12 and had two younger brothers. Our family enjoyed a happy rapport with our Maori neighbours, a number of whom were local farmers, while others lived at the nearby Kawerau pa.

Mrs Konu came from the pa every fruit season with a huge flax kit full of freshly picked fruit. She would softly explain to our mother, 'I tell my family I am going to take my first fruit to Mrs Robertson.' Mother had a great affection for Mrs Konu and they enjoyed afternoon tea together before Mrs Konu left to walk back to her home.

During Christmas 1934, my city relatives from Auckland were expected to spend time with us on the farm so Mother had baked and baked and baked in the coal range oven. She had also transformed the garden into a welcoming display. The garden paths and those around the house were made of Tarawera ash, which resembled extremely fine gravel.

On Christmas Day my excited mother rose at dawn to garden-rake the paths free of all our footprints and eventually they showed only the precise long lines made by her skill with the rake. Our good-humoured

Lunch-break during haymaking. My mother is standing by the tree and my father is second from the left.

father and we children were forbidden to use those pathways until our visitors had arrived.

Mother woke me at dawn: 'Belle, wake up. Look out your window.' What I saw and heard has remained with me all my life. There in the home paddock, and closely surrounding our house, was a group of Maori joyously singing Christmas carols. Their mellow and beautiful voices wafted on the clear rural air and enriched the countryside, and our lives.

Our family felt deeply honoured on that incomparable Christmas morning.

Our kitchen sink

Patricia Ridding

WHEN WE WERE married in 1949 our worldly goods consisted of two easy chairs, a radio, linen, china and a small bank account. We saved carefully for the day when we could buy our own home and if 2/6 was left over from housekeeping it was put in the Post Office Savings Bank. Our little nest egg grew slowly and in 1950 we had the opportunity to buy a furnished house in Miramar, with a rehab loan available to returned servicemen.

Our three-bedroom house with spacious lawn and room for a vegetable garden was our pride and joy – except for the kitchen! It was a small room with a tiny window, a copper tub, stove, a few cupboards and a sink with an old wooden surround. A board over the tub served as a baking and dishing up area and for as long as there were only two of us we managed well, but six years and two children later our kitchen was a daily problem. One day the plumber came to fix our rusty taps and gave us the name of a builder who did renovations at a reasonable cost. Over the next two weeks our back porch was enclosed, cupboards and a large window installed, and to my great delight, a green Beatty washing machine with a wringer arrived for our new laundry. Now all that was needed to complete our kitchen was a new sink, but a stainless steel one was way beyond our budget.

At this time, Wellington Airport was being developed and all the houses in Rongotai Terrace had been relocated or demolished as the hill was removed. Our ever-helpful and enterprising builder suggested I ring a Petone demolition yard on the slim chance they had a suitable sink and bench from one of those demolished houses. To our great surprise there was one. The right measurements, stainless steel, almost new, and at a price we could afford. The only problem was that it had to be picked up that morning.

The trusty Morris Minor with Pat Ridding and passengers, Christine and Graham.

Now the fun began! We had a Morris Minor car and I had a new driver's licence and two small children. The thought of that lovely sink waiting for me overcame any fear and trepidation so I bundled the children into the car and bravely set off. I told my three-year-old not to speak from the time we passed Point Jerningham lighthouse at Oriental Bay until we saw the trains at the railway station. I didn't want any distractions on my first drive through city traffic with the children. However, we reached Petone after an uneventful drive along the Hutt Road and were met with disbelief at the demolition yard when I said I'd come for the sink bench. If the boss had known me he would not have said, 'You'll never fit it in there.' He didn't realise how my determination made all things possible. After much heaving and pushing, and with the front passenger seat down, I was ready to drive home with the bench aboard. The children were wedged in – I didn't tell them not to move – they couldn't have!

Our drive home was completed without mishap and by the time my husband came home our new sink bench was installed.

The opening of Wellington Airport in October 1959 was held on a bleak, windy day, and we marvelled at the planes and shared the thrill of seeing the RAF Vulcan bomber that tipped its wing on the runway and had to fly on to Ohakea. But in spite of all the excitement, I couldn't help looking over to where the houses of Rongotai Terrace used to be and remembering how we got our new kitchen sink.

Meals and grandmas

Dorothy Black

I'VE NEVER LIKED tripe and onions but from time to time I've had to eat it when out visiting and sometimes it has been delicious. There's a knack to cooking tripe. It takes a very long time and the tripe needs to be cut into very small pieces. I think parsley went into it too and good cooks seem to be able to make it all very edible. After all, what's the difference between tripe and heart, brains, kidney or liver? Or what about the Scotsman's much loved haggis?

Memories of tripe take me back to the cooking of my grandmother's day. She was a wonderful cook on the old coal range. She

290 Taranaki Street, Wellington.

always had a kettle of hot water ready for a hot drink and the soup pot never seemed to be empty, always simmering for hungry new arrivals. Often she had a dish of dried peas, and goodness knows how long that was cooked, ready to be mashed up with lashings of butter, pepper and salt. And the most luscious milk-cocoa I've ever had. My mouth waters at the memory, even after all these years.

Grandmother's monster of a stove was rarely out, only when she had to clean it and blacken everything in sight. It was set into a wall, with very little light for her to see what she was doing.

I've often tried to turn out food like hers but have never succeeded. If I left soup on the stove as long as she did, it would become inedible, but she seemed to keep adding to it and adding to it and it always tasted fresh and appetising.

My grandmother – my father's mother – was well over 80 when I was a girl. My brother and I were lucky to have two grandmothers. During the school holidays we always spent one day a week with my mother's mother who was about 20 years younger than my other Gran. This grandmother didn't turn out food like the first one, but she was a dab hand at making hot scones at the drop of a hat and she taught me how to. She spoilt us in quite a different way. At lunch-time she'd say, 'What do you two want to eat. Fish and chips or a meat pie?' Then she'd trot us up to the nearby shops to buy our choice.

When we got home that night mother would demand, 'Well, what rubbish did you have to eat today?' And then, with a sniff, she'd add, 'At her age she really should know better!'

But we loved it because that was the only time we were allowed to eat such 'rubbish'!

Bags of uses

Jean Williams

MANY DECADES AGO flour was delivered to the home in either 25 or 50-pound bags and the bigger bags had many uses.

Back in nineteen twenty-two
The thing that we all had to do
Was use whatever was available
And turn it into something saleable.
The bags in which we bought our flour
Gave us work for many an hour.
Unpicked and washed to oust the brand,
The whitened calico was grand.
Some destined for those pretty aprons
Became the pride of many matrons
Others graced a little table
Bleached as well as we were able.
With a coloured piece of print
One took the economic hint,
And made a useful pillowcase,
On someone's bed to find a place.
Some ended up as rag doll toys,
Or lined the pants of little boys.

But you can certainly be sure
Their useful future was secure.

Sugar bags came from the grocer in 70-pound bags and were made of a
hemp-like material in a fairly firm weave.

Dad tipped the sugar in the bin
Its weight was not too much for him
Then Mother took the bag away
To use it in a different way.
Unpicked and laundered, its new life
Was destined by the careful wife.
More bags than one she needed for
A mat to grace the polished floor.
Oven cloths came next to mind
The simple, common, garden kind,
To protect fingers from the heat
When dishing up those roasts of meat.
The apron worn for Monday's wash
Was made of sugar bag. By gosh!
With pocket like a kangaroo
The pegs would be right there for you.
Before the use of stainless steel,
We cleaned knives after every meal,
Rubbed between two bits of bag
They shone – but what a boring fag.
When we'd packed those goodies for

The young men serving in the war
The tins were soldered good and fast
And sewed in sugar bag at last.

Kerosene tins were plentiful in those days and were not wasted either.

The kerosene for heat and light
Came in tins all shining bright
But when the final drop was drained
The empty tin for use remained.
The fencing wire, your number eight
A handle made to carry weight
Then of course we all were able to
Use them in the byre or stable.
Milk or water, oats or chaff
Coal or tatties, that's not half
The many things those tins did hold
They were so versatile, I'm told.
Cut lengthwise and then opened up
In them we washed both plate and cup
And on the other half remaining
Those dishes could be left for draining.
So let us then salute the way those tins
Found uses yesterday.
They were really quite fantastic
Now of course we all use plastic.

Beside a Hawke's Bay river in 1931.

Summer picnics

Valerie Smith

SUMMER HOLIDAYS TODAY, New Zealand-style – families stuff the car with clothes, food, toys, books, swimming gear and the dog, maybe Granny too, and head for the beach, lake or river. Some will camp, or blob out in a motel or holiday home, while others relax in that marvellous Kiwi icon – the family bach or crib. That fibrolite or wood creation with unmatched windows and long-past-their-best crockery and furniture; where nobody minds sand on the floor or sagging mattresses.

But for many families, in the 1930s and 40s, when my generation was young, such holidays never happened. For a while we were the children of 'hard times' who, thanks to the Depression, the Second World War and large families, had no chance of holidays with our parents. Occasionally, I feel sad and a little deprived, as I see my children and their families drive away with all their gear. But then I remember, with a rush of warmth and nostalgia, the Christmas holidays of my own childhood when, even without a car, telephone or money to spare for luxuries, the summers were long, golden and utterly happy. I suppose it did rain sometimes and I suppose we children squabbled, got sick or resented doing the chores, but we were far too busy making the most of every precious hour to waste time being miserable.

There was so much to cram into six weeks' holiday. First, the Christmas shopping. Half a crown was enough for gifts for all the family. We made our own decorations and cards, helped mix the cake and pudding, and shelled the freshly picked peas. After Christmas we had five whole weeks to play, long hours to read, build houses and huts, climb trees, play make-believe and stretch the imagination in any direction. We were always outside, returning reluctantly only for chores and meals, then, drunk with sunshine and exercise of mind and body, we'd fall content into bed and be instantly asleep.

Although confined to our own neighbourhoods and the limits of our imaginations we weren't deprived of all outings. There were occasional holidays to relatives and sometimes trips to town or the pictures. And we had picnics. The best was our Boxing Day picnic. Whole families drove down to the beach where mothers and aunts sat on deck chairs in the shade while fathers with rolled-up trouser legs and straw hats supervised our paddling, swimming and ball games. When cars disappeared during the Depression Grandfather decided that we should continue this special picnic – by walking to the beach. We had a very early start to get the farm chores finished first, then we loaded extra food and clothes around the babies in the pram and pushchair. Dad shouldered his haversack filled with ginger beer, buckets and spades. We tucked our togs and towels under our arms, jammed large sunhats on our heads and we were off down the long dusty road to the beach. We met up with the other families on the way and we children rushed ahead, playing games until we reached the narrow shingle beach that was 'paradise'.

A glorious lunch was topped off with mince pies and Christmas cake washed down with warm ginger beer, and we cleaned our teeth with the first of the new season's apples. All too soon the sun was low and we had to leave for home – the hills seemed steeper, the road longer. There were no games on the way home, just a patient plod. Home, so eagerly abandoned that morning, now became a haven and our beds twice as sweet.

There were other picnics, of course, but I remember those Boxing Day ones with such affection because in those dark days such treats were simple and rare so every moment was to be savoured and treasured forever. Even today the smell of wet togs on warm shingle, the taste of ginger beer and soggy tomato sandwiches and the sight of children with floppy sunhats all stir memories so sweet they're almost painful.

What a racket!

Neil Todd

I WAS SITTING on the veranda enjoying the afternoon sun and complaining about the racket of those skateboards going up and down the footpath when my memory was jogged back more than 50 years. As a young boy in 1946 I decided to make a trolley. Materials were hard to find so my trolley consisted of the bare necessities, which I'd obtained by fair, or perhaps dubious, means. I'd sneaked into Dad's shed, found a pair of axles and asked Dad if he had any wheels. 'I might need those axles,' was the stern reply, 'and I've told you to stay out of the shed when I'm not around.' I hung my head and said I was sorry but asked again if he had any wheels.

A couple of days later Dad produced four cast-iron wheels asking if these were what I was looking for and what was I going to do with them? I told him I was going to make a trolley and did he have any spare wood like that long piece around the back of the shed? I only wanted a piece off the end, but I was threatened with banishment if I even thought of cutting up Dad's painting plank and I'd better look elsewhere for my wood.

Somehow, after desperate searching, and from places undisclosed, I acquired the necessary wood to make the base to fix the axles onto. 'Have you any bolts, Dad?' He gave me a wry smile, knowing I wouldn't be put off that easily, and produced a long bolt with a nut rusted on the end. It might do to swivel the front axle on for steering. Dad gave me a pair of pliers and a spanner and said I could use the bolt if I could undo the nut. It took some hours after school to undo that nut but I won and then Dad produced a drop of oil to make the nut run up the thread easily. Tongue in cheek, I asked Dad if he had any washers. He shook his head, but went back into the shed and came out with a tin of washers. The four washers completed the fitting of the front axle to the main body of the trolley.

Now all that remained was to fit the rear axle and the wheels. I inspected my mates' trolleys to see how they'd fitted on the rear axle. Bent nails seemed to do the trick with a couple of large staples hammered in. 'Dad, do you have any nails or staples?' He had only bent nails that had to be straightened. I hit my fingers a few times in the process but soon I had some straight nails and began to fit the rear axles. With Dad's help they were fitted and the wheels put on, held in place by nails used as cotter pins. We tied a piece of rope to the front axle to steer it by, then carried out tests up and down the path. All seemed well, except a box as a seat would be better. Mr Foulks the grocer had a wooden box but for him to part with it meant I had to clean out the storeroom at the back of the shop, which took a couple of days' work after school, but eventually I had my wooden seat. More nails were straightened, the seat fitted, and my trolley was ready for street trials.

Our street had a perfect hill to race our trolleys on and my mates and I gathered after school, when chores and jobs for Mum had been completed, and raced till Dad's whistle announced it was time to come home. Modifications to the fitting on the rear axle meant I needed some larger staples. These were found in the structure of the neighbour's chicken run, which, incidentally, didn't fall over after their removal – it just leaned a little. I remember Dad checked our fence when he found these staples on my trolley, and quizzed me on how I'd acquired them. He never believed they were 'just found'. The dripping from the Sunday roast greased the axles. We raced after school on a regular basis and competition was fierce and not without cuts, grazes and bruises. That didn't matter to racing drivers. But torn clothes meant Mum was after you – and that was frightening.

I can still see Mrs Mac banging on the window and shaking her fist at us for making all that noise as we raced down the hill then pulled our trolleys back up to do it all again. I remember thinking what a crabby lady she was. Later I found out that she was then a night nursing sister at the hospital, so I suppose she was trying to sleep. Still, I wish those damn kids and their skateboards would go somewhere else today to make all that racket.

Baroona from Waiheke

Tom Briggs

I LIVED ON Waiheke Island until I was 13 and I remember one very severe storm that affected the ferries to Auckland. When the *Baroona* arrived at the island she couldn't dock at the wharf and had to drop anchor to ride out the storm. During the night she dragged her anchor and cut the main power cable to the island. When the power was out my Dad uncovered an old coal range, which was behind a wall panel, he lit the Tilley lamps and dug out the primus. The power wasn't restored for three or four weeks – and it was in the middle of winter!

While this storm was still blowing we had to go to Auckland. Normally *Baroona* took one and a half hours, but this would be a long trip and one I'll never forget – it was the roughest trip I've ever been on. One minute we were going up the waves, then next down them, then the boat would corkscrew before going up again. Before long the captain ordered everybody to go into the cabins and stay there. We were also told to shut all the portholes and doors and not to open them as the water was pouring in. The captain called for men to take turns on the pumps.

The vicar from Waiheke was on board and got everybody together, sitting or kneeling, and he called for a few minutes of prayer asking that we would make it safely to port without injury or loss of life. I remember my brother and sister telling Mum that we didn't want to die.

The *Baroona* with the *English Star* in the background.
Wilkinson Collection, *Alexander Turnbull Library of New Zealand,*
Te Puna Matauranga o Aotearoa F-10574-1/4

She held all of us together and said that nothing would happen to us, because the vicar said so, and that we'd soon be in Auckland. When we finally reached Auckland, *Baroona* couldn't get into King's Wharf and had to go to the Devonport naval base. The dockyard staff said that if she hadn't been built as a cargo boat, capable of sailing on the open seas, she'd have sunk with all the water she'd taken on board. Not surprisingly, *Baroona* had to stay at Devonport for repairs. After that trip Mum always asked the passengers getting off the ferry at Waiheke what the crossing had been like before she bought her tickets.

I've been back to Waiheke many times but I've never had another trip as rough as that day on the old *Baroona*.

Our whippet

Betty Mollgaard

WHEN I WAS a child in Palmerston North our family transport was the pushbike. Dad had a tall, upstanding Eadie Coaster with a three-speed gear change on the bar. The pedals were steel with saw-edge grips – no good for children's feet – so we children never touched the 'giraffe', as we called it. When I was small I rode on a seat on the bar with my toes resting on the forks. I hated it because I always felt very insecure and I held onto the handlebars with a vice-like grip. My greatest delight came when I was almost six years old and got a brand-new bike for my second year at school.

Besides picnics and exploring the countryside, we made an annual bicycle foray to the Makerua swamp to pick blackberries – big, luscious, juicy ones! We set off early, armed with billycans and kerosene tins, to ride the nine miles towards Shannon on roads which weren't sealed, and were just three ruts divided by piles of loose metal. I tried to cross over and fell off, leaving one handlebar buried in the metal, and how I cried because I thought I'd broken my new bike. After picking all day we walked our laden bicycles back to Shannon to catch the Field's Express back to Palmerston North. The train had been named after politician William Field who had pushed for a daily service between Palmerston North and Wellington.

We loved the blackberry and apple pies and the blackberry jam. One year Mother attempted to make blackberry wine in an old wash jug, but while the jug was perched on a shelf in the wash-house with the brew ready for bottling it was knocked off and the wine flowed out the door and over the porch, turning the concrete floor a rich purple. We smelled like a winery for ages and the mess attracted the flies, which then sat in a drunken stupor all over the floor. Mother never tried wine-making again.

In 1929 my father bought a Whippet four-door sedan for about £290 – a luxury when wages were about £6 a week. The salesman gave Dad driving lessons and one day, after being sworn to silence, I was allowed to sit on the back seat during a lesson. We were driving along an empty back road when the instructor suddenly shouted, 'There's a cow! Stop!' I couldn't see a cow and decided grown-ups were mad. The Whippet gave us great joy because we could travel so far. Dad decided to visit his family in Dunedin and we prepared to camp on the way. First Dad made a strong green canvas bag that held four suitcases on the roof. Inside the car he hinged the front seats so that they would drop down to form beds for Mum and me, and he slung a hammock on the outside running boards for himself and my brother. When we were travelling, the long hammock poles, a kerosene primus and spare petrol were lashed to the running board on the passenger's side. Mother made a calico tent, which completely covered the car and was pegged down at each side. But one drawback was that the tent had to be completely dismantled before we could use the car!

On the Kaikoura coast road we had to negotiate road works and a large heap of rubble in the middle of the road. One night we camped at the Rangitata Bridge. Dad was a great believer in daily ablutions and plunged into the river's milky waters. He nearly froze solid. We didn't know that the milky look came from the river being snow-fed! I remember a massive thunderstorm at Ashburton – with lightning, hail

Our evening meal. The camp is set up, showing the home-made tent.

and heavy rain. After visiting our relations in Dunedin we returned to Palmerston North in spite of the neighbours' dire forebodings that we'd never survive such a hazardous overseas trip.

The Whippet had one very bad habit – she broke back axles. Dad always carried a spare in the tool kit under the back seat. One time Dad had jacked up the car and was fishing about for the broken piece when a frisky young bull turned up. Dad was so engrossed that when the bull came right up and sniffed at him he just waved his hand and told it to go away! The bull put its horn under the car bumper and gave it a jolt – which released the broken part – then trotted back up the road. I'm sure it was laughing!

All on a summer's day

Judy Hannan

I STOOD ON the lino-covered floor in the kitchen while my mother combed the knots out of my fine straight hair. I savoured the coolness under my bare feet. I was eager to be outside, to run across the grass, through the dandelions and put a buttercup under my chin to see if I liked butter. With my sunbonnet tied under my chin and a clean handkerchief tucked into my pinny pocket I was ready for the sights, the sounds and the freedom of an early summer's day. Soon I was off down the hill, through the orchard and onto the gate, which squeaked as it swung to and fro. From Clinkard's farm across the road I could hear the ducks quacking and hens squabbling for their grain. The bread van was coming, changing gear nosily as it laboured up the hill. The next delivery was a raised tin loaf and half a wholemeal to the house just beyond the gate. I spelled out the letters, B-U-C-H-A-N-A-N. One day soon I'd know how to say that word! I never tried to say it out loud at home because everyone laughed.

After looking carefully to the left, then to the right, I crossed the road, and felt the muddy water in the ditch squelch between my bare toes. There was tall, hollow-stemmed grass which could be picked and put to your lips to make a satisfying whistling sound. Mother had told me that this was as far as I could go, so I sat on the warm grass, listening to the bees buzzing in and out of nodding poppies and snapdragons in the garden behind me. A bus lumbered past. An easy word to spell: K-E-Y-S – Keys. Two people were coming towards me. I knew them. One pair of good, black lady's shoes and one pair of good, black, well-polished men's shoes – Grandma and Grandpa. I swung along between them and Grandma asked, 'Where are your boots, child?' I'd heard this question many times and always gave the same answer: 'They're at home.'

'I always wore my boots when I was a little girl,' Grandma remarked. We passed through the top gate to the front door where Mother waited to greet us. An aroma of cheese scones baking meant lunch wasn't far away. From among the reading glasses, string kit, fancy cottons, scissors and crochet hook in Grandma's shopping bag appeared a brown paper parcel tied with string. Who was it for? Mother smiled knowingly. Grandpa winked. In the parcel were a pencil, a notebook, two new handkerchiefs and an embroidered pinny. Guess who was starting school next day? Grandma and Grandpa had come to visit to share my last golden day of freedom before the rigid timetables of school life.

Speaking from memory

Dawn Sheppard

AT THE CLOSE of the 1945 school year I entered the impromptu speech competitions for the senior school. House points were at stake! Each entrant was called into an empty classroom and left, for two or three minutes, to face the topic written on the blackboard, which turned out to be 'The Most Important Day Of My Life'. We found out afterwards that we had all chosen 'The Day the War Ended'.

The competition was held in our Wellington East Girls' College assembly hall with all the school as the audience and the judges sitting at tables well back in the auditorium. I stumbled through my speech, jerkily describing the assembly at which we'd been told of Japan's surrender and had then been dismissed three days early for the rest of the term. After giving my speech I tried to work out why I'd not been able to make matchless oratory from this opportunity. With all the wisdom of a 16-year-old I decided that I'd been distracted. The assembly hall and the rows of people had awakened another set of memories that interfered with what I was trying to say about that day in August 1945.

The memories were from six years earlier, December 1939, and that other hall was unpainted, unlined and deep in the south-east Otago bush country. The rows of people were parents from the farms, railway houses and sawmills – the young and the old from miles around. It was the Maclennan School concert and as the school had fewer than 30 children much of the concert depended on repeat performances by older children who led and shepherded the overwhelmed juniors. In a grass skirt, and inexpertly twirling pois, I sang *Pokarekare Ana* and *E Pari Ra*. I then changed into my sister's highland dancing costume and presented *The Skye Boat Song*. Dressed as a gypsy Casanova I was the villain in that lushly sentimental tableau of betrayed maidenhood, *Do Not Trust him Gentle Lady*. The maiden I betrayed was in Standard 6 and I was in Standard 4. She was well developed, had red hair and was a foot taller than I was! As part of a 'backing trio' I sang *The Wedding of the Painted Doll* in which all the infants took part as members of a large wedding party. They enchanted the audience. The bridegroom was a terrified six-year-old blonde boy, the bride being a dainty, dark-eyed little girl who loved the part. I had secretly cherished that role for myself. Then I was a black mammy in a play for which we wore black woollen stocking tops over our heads with suitably embroidered eye and mouth holes cut out.

Then there was a play, written by our two teachers, about village personalities – the bachelor storekeeper, and the spinster boarding-house owner. Their status provided enough for a plot. The exact story line has long gone from memory but this glimpse of local romance delighted everyone there that night.

Little Hugh, from the infant class, was A. A. Milne's John.

John had great big waterproof boots on.
John had a great big waterproof hat
'And that', said John, 'is that'.

It had taken two teachers and several of the older pupils weeks to imprint those few words in Hugh's mind! But he performed all that was required of him on the night. A solid little boy, round faced, blue eyed, with dark curls under his oversized hat – he'd have charmed any audience.

As soon as the concert was over the audience exploded into action. The windows were opened and the seating forms were passed outside. Tilley lamps were pumped up, the floor was sprinkled with French chalk and a pianist began thumping out a circular waltz. Everyone danced – even the teachers and our parents! Then came the special children's dance. Quite formally, I was asked to dance by a strong, handsome 20-year-old bushman, much sought after by the local girls. Somehow we got through the figures of the dance, led, pushed or carried to the right spots at the right times. Exhausted, I was escorted back to my seat against the wall. 'You were very good, you must have done this before,' said my partner. I swelled with delight. I was in a state of instant, pure, unqualified happiness.

There wasn't another concert at Maclennan for the next six years because of the war. The war seemed to be a faraway event, distant and unreal to us in our corner of the New Zealand bush. But the memories of a 10-year-old, and the inarticulate thoughts of a 16-year-old have stood the test of time.

God save the Queen

Adrienne Frater

AUNTY OLA PRESSED my Brownie uniform twice and sprinkled water onto the yellow tie to iron it flat. I was going to see the Queen on her 1953 royal tour. I'd cut the fairy-tale 'Elizabeth Regina' out of *The Weekly News* and pasted her four times into my Christmas scrapbook with flour and water. I might see the Duke too. I had my written instructions from Brown Owl, and Uncle Roy was going to 'dub' me into town on his bike, at quarter past seven. He left me outside St Paul's, and after she'd counted 12 heads, Brown Owl took us to our waiting spot just outside Wanganui's Cook's Gardens' gate. An old man wearing medals gave us paper Union Jacks, and we waited. Guides and Scouts at the back; Brownies and Cubs in front. Badges shining and berets on straight, we stood in the sun and waited. Red, white and blue flags danced across the street. A big picture of the Queen and Duke sat on top of a hydrangea and fern arch. I stood on one leg and then the other.

Brown Owl gave us orange quarters to suck. 'Don't drip the juice!' she ordered. A Cub pushed in front of me so I gave him a poke. 'Adrienne, get in line, they're coming,' snapped Brown Owl, flicking her eyes over her 12 mushroom heads. I waved and waved. Nothing happened. I waved some more and suddenly the crowd gave a big push. I waved my flag faster and called out 'God Save the Queen', as a big, black open-top car drove close. My tummy fluttered. I felt something

The civic reception at Pukekura Park, New Plymouth, for Queen Elizabeth II and Prince Philip, Duke of Edinburgh, January 1954.
Photographer E.P. Christensen. *Alexander Turnbull Library of New Zealand, Te Puna Matauranga o Aotearoa F–42140-1/2*

grip my Brownie belt and hold me steady. I stood on the tips of my lace-up shoes and leaned forward. I looked for her wavy dark hair, her queenly smile, and her sparkly dress. I could see the Duke's head. I could see a little white hat. I could see a waving white hand. I pushed forward and yelled, 'God Save the Queen'.

The man unhooked his walking stick from my belt and smiled. 'Did you see the Queen?'

'I saw her hat.'

On the ferries

Jillian Burcher

FOR PEOPLE WHO live on the North Shore, the Auckland ferries are a unique way of life. In the 1950s we lived on a farm in Chivalry Road and the service we used was the one from Bayswater. Later, when I lived in Takapuna and started work in the city, I travelled through Devonport. The ferries were double-ended and had saucer-shaped bottoms, which were necessary on the Bayswater run. Shoal Bay is shallow and even with a marked, dredged channel the ferry sometimes ran aground at low spring tides, and then had to dislodge itself. The Bayswater run was across the prevailing westerly winds and sometimes the boat rolled so much my mother had to hold onto my skirt to save me sliding off the seat. A common sight was the ferry coming in to berth with an alarming list as a full load of passengers sheltered from a bad westerly wind, but somehow the ferries never capsized. A number of passengers never bothered to sit inside during the journey, and in the winter they tended to congregate around the funnel in the centre of the upper deck where it was warmer. The ferries were coal-fired, so if anyone intended to sit out there it was a good idea to consider which way the wind was blowing – to avoid soot from the funnel.

The last ferry left the city about 12.30 in the morning. Then the night launch took over. Regular commuters who travelled at peak times every morning and evening had their favourite seats – almost as if they were reserved. Woe betide anyone who took another person's seat – they usually got a very black look.

We were a group of four or five girls who travelled to work on the eight o'clock morning ferry from Devonport. When it was wet we sat inside in the lower stern cabin on the starboard side. When it was fine we sat outside, but on the same side. A short, thickset fellow often sat opposite us and he caught my eye because he seemed to have a head that was too large for the rest of him. He was later to have a big hand in my future – he was Robert Muldoon. He wasn't the only future prime minister to travel on the ferries during the 1950s. Norman Kirk was once a stoker.

A regular event on our morning trip was the departure of the Tasman Empire Airways Limited Solent flying boat, which left from Mechanics Bay for Sydney. After the flying boats stopped we watched other aircraft service the islands in the Hauraki Gulf.

I usually managed to catch the 5.15 ferry home. I'd sit in the upper forward cabin and read the *Auckland Star*, which I'd bought on my way down Queen Street. Outside the ferry building there was a little cart that sold hot roasted nuts, and one that sold flowers, so sometimes I'd buy a little something to take home to my mother.

Royal visit 1927

Alice Evans

IN THE LATE 1920s I was attending Epsom Girls' Grammar School in Auckland. One great highlight was the visit of the Duke and Duchess of York in February 1927. They arrived in Auckland on the battle cruiser HMS *Renown*. It was a grey, drizzling morning and a group of us in school uniform and raincoats hurried down Parnell Road and took a short cut over Constitution Hill where we could see over the harbour. It was alive with vessels. Then we had our first glimpse of that grey shape coming round North Head to the sound of gun salutes and sirens. We hurried down to Princes Street wharf to a lookout position, which had been arranged for members of the Navy League. As we got closer we were slowed down by the mass of people so we linked arms, shuffled sideways and then finally burst through to the wharf, up the steep companionway steps and onto the open flat roof. There was *Renown*, in all her majesty, and then the barge flying the royal ensign heading for Admiralty Steps.

As I hurried down to join the street procession I took one last backwards look and fell over a heap of fine metal on the rooftop taking out both knees of my black woollen stockings. But with my raincoat torn and both knees bleeding and full of gravel I hurried on through the crowds lining the pavements. People were hanging out of windows and

Three room-mates
in school uniform.

crouching on shop verandas – and there were wet flags and decorations everywhere. Then our dainty Duchess passed – in a powder blue cloche hat and blue brocade coat with a high silver-grey collar. She smiled and waved from the open vehicle, taking no notice of the rain. She was so lovely we hardly noticed the Duke!

Then they were gone. Battered and still bleeding, I worked my way back to the school hostel where I had to endure the removal of the bits of gravel and the stinging friar's balsam on my knees!

But we had a fine day for the children's display in the Auckland Domain and I had the thrill of being close enough to the Duchess to take in her wonderful complexion, blue eyes and endearing smile. I was so close I could have touched the pompom on her hat.

I was one of the lucky ones – my family in the far north, like many others, had to be content with the photographs in the next *Weekly News*.

My hermit

Jim Closs

GINGE, SO-CALLED because of the colour of his hair and beard, lived in an isolated bush clearing about 10 miles north of Murchison on the eastern side of the Buller River. His shack was about the size of a single garage and had an iron roof, black plastic walls and a flap for a door. There were no windows and at one end there was an open fire for cooking and warmth. Furniture was primitive – a bed, table and chair, and several boxes piled on top of each other for his belongings and food. Ginge was a gold miner and it was said he had a large cache hidden somewhere but, as far as I know, it has never been found. Ginge was one of the most contented people I have ever met. He didn't seem to have a care in the world. The director of the Social Welfare Department in Nelson asked me to call on Ginge on my monthly field officer visits to Murchison and over the years I got to know him very well. What surprised me was that he always seemed to know which day I'd visit even though he had no calendar, newspaper, wireless or watch.

Ginge was a wonderful teller of tales and I heard many of them. He would look at me with his pale blue eyes, which never wavered, and what he related sounded almost authentic! For instance, he said he was the man who persuaded the Canadian Pacific railways to use a wider gauge track. He said he had cycled across northern Canada. He told me that after he died, a plane, to be sent by the American military in Perth, would collect his body for burial there. This was for services rendered to the American forces during the war. But I knew that Ginge had never been out of New Zealand.

I normally called on Ginge in the morning and on one visit I arrived at his shack and there was no sign of him. The flap was down and no smoke came from the chimney. I called out and a weak voice asked, 'Is that you, Mr Closs?'

I went in and found a very sick man in bed, he'd been waiting a long time for me to visit. I made him comfortable, and went to Murchison for help. On my next Murchison visit I found Ginge happily settled in the local hospital. The local people decided Ginge couldn't return to his shack and the Forestry Department donated a one-man hut, which they transported, free, to a site not far from the old man's shack.

When Ginge died I was overseas and I was sorry to miss his funeral. However I went to the cemetery and found his headstone, which was simply inscribed 'Ginge'.

No plane had come from Perth and I said farewell to my hermit.

Christmas at Ruakituri Valley in 1936

Tom Spence

MY MOTHER BEGAN baking a couple of weeks before Christmas on her wood range. She made a large Christmas cake as well as shortbread and small cakes, and so only the best dry manuka would do! Grandfather, whom everyone knew as 'Boss', was in sole charge of our vegetable garden and many months before Christmas he'd planted peas, beans and potatoes to be ready for the great day. On Christmas morning, large buckets of these fresh new vegetables were brought in from the garden and later that same morning we had to wash the potatoes while someone else did the beans and peas. We liked helping to prepare the peas, and quite a few didn't make it to the saucepan! We got fresh mint from the creek to be chopped for the sauce.

Dad would kill a well-fattened lamb a couple of days earlier. It was the hottest time of the year and blowflies were really bad, but they didn't move about after sundown, so we youngsters took the torch and shone it for Dad to kill the lamb. It was then covered with a large meat bag made from old sheeting and left overnight hanging in a tree to 'set'. Dad had to be up early before the flies to collect the lamb and cut it up, or 'cut it down' as most people said.

On Christmas Eve we'd leave pillowslips made from 50-pound

flour bags at the ends of our beds and on Christmas morning everyone was up with the larks – but no one ever saw Santa! The pillowslips were filled with goodies, tin tip-trucks with wind-up motors, marbles and, one year, a spinning top. And there was always a book. One year we got a Meccano set and little trucks and cars were taken up to the 'roads' we'd made along a clay bank above the house. Our imaginations knew no bounds.

About 11 in the morning the visitors began arriving. Grandmother and Granddad, Uncle and Auntie Burridge and their daughters with their husbands. Fourteen of us would sit down to a midday meal. With no electricity our mother had cooked all the meats, made a huge steamed pudding in a large flour bag, fruit salad, trifles and jellies. Our long wooden table, with a white sheet spread on it, seated everyone. We all knew Granddad put the threepences and buttons in the steamed pudding, which was served with lovely soft custard.

Before afternoon tea we all had a swim in the Ruakituri River, some of us in sugar-bag togs, which filled with water and almost drowned us! Then we caught our horses and showed off to our town relatives by jumping our horses over the eight-wire fences. We were pupils at the local native school so we also entertained our guests with Maori action songs and the finale was the haka! The visitors set out for home just after four in the afternoon and, before long, we would be sitting down to a meal of the leftovers!

Sunday school lesson in 1947

Neill Todd

AS I SET out for Sunday school Mum gave me a sixpence for my tram fares and threepence for the collection with the parting words that I was to come straight home after the service. My tram pulled up and I noticed that it was number 243 – one of my favourites – and as I climbed aboard a head popped out of the motorman's cab: my uncle Jim was the driver that day. He invited me to stand in the driver's cab and opened the offside door to let me stand alongside him. I was delighted at such luck and told him I was on my way to Sunday school. I watched as he released the air brakes and moved the power control handle slowly forward as the tram moved off. There were several stops before I had to get off and I stood very still as Uncle Jim talked about the family, but my attention was really on the tracks in front of us and what Uncle Jim was doing. When we came to my stop Uncle Jim asked if I'd like to go on with him to Point Chevalier and then back to Three Kings? I needed no prompting to agree and looked straight ahead as we went past my Sunday school feeling sure God would punish me for my erring ways, but it was a chance I was prepared to take.

The tram went on into town, picking up passengers along the way, and as we headed down a long hill Uncle Jim told me to turn the big wheel in front of me which applied the braking to the tracks. Cautiously I turned it and we steadily went downhill, then round a bend where I was told to unwind the wheel to let off the braking system. As we neared the centre of town Uncle Jim said I had to sit inside the tram in case an inspector got on, but once through the town I could go back to the motorman's cab. I sat quietly with the other passengers, still feeling a little guilty about Sunday school, but I was soon back in the cab watching the tracks and enjoying the sway of the tram. It was exciting going over the points and round the bends because the front of the tram appeared to go way past the turn before it lurched round and went in the right direction.

Soon we headed down Point Chevalier Road and arrived at the terminus where we prepared for the return journey. I helped Uncle Jim disengage the tram pole from the bracket on the roof and then we removed the braking handle and I was allowed to carry the power control handle from one end of the tram to the other – to the new 'front end' of the tram. Soon it was time to go. The conductor clanged the bell, Uncle Jim pushed on the power control as he released the air brakes, and we moved off. As we rode through town I had to sit with the other passengers again but when we reached the safety zone at the top of Symonds Street the conductor let me back into the cab with Uncle Jim. As we went along Mt Eden Road, Uncle Jim took my hand and together we moved the power control handle forwards to make the tram speed up, and then eased it back when we came to a bend. It was an experience most boys only dreamed about.

When we got near Sunday school I was worried they might have finished early and I'd be found out. I even thought of asking God for help but changed my mind, knowing I was probably in trouble with Him anyway! At my home stop I thanked Uncle Jim and headed home.

Mum commented that I was home early and as I changed out of my good clothes I hid my threepence, promising God I'd put it into the collection next Sunday.

I spent the week worrying that my friends might ask where I'd been last Sunday and that Mum might hear. 'Were you sick last Sunday?' asked our teacher. I hung my head and nodded. I felt sure God was watching me – so I put my two threepences into the collection.

A couple of weeks later Mum looked at me in a funny way and said she'd heard that they'd had a lesson on trams at Sunday school the other week. I quickly grabbed the coal bucket.

'I'll get some more coal in, Mum', and I headed for the woodshed.

That awesome veil

Joyce Powell

THEY'RE PART OF history now, those awesome, starched, white veils some registered nurses used to wear. I first met that impressive headgear during the school holidays when my mother took my youngest brother to see the Plunket nurse. It was very common in the thirties and forties for the clinic to be part of the local ladies' rest rooms and I remember it smelled of disinfectant. Before we walked through the door my mother said, 'Behave yourselves in front of the Plunket nurse.' We weren't the best-behaved children in town, but she needn't have worried because there was no question of us playing up, or speaking out of turn, in front of the awesome veil that covered the nurse's hair. I watched my brother being weighed on the scales, imagining the Plunket nurse pedalling her bike around the streets, visiting homes with her veil blowing out behind her like a sail. How did she keep it on when it was windy? Then Mum told me she didn't wear a veil when she was home visiting. She wore a grey hat. What a disappointment – a hat wouldn't be nearly as impressive.

The next time I met up with an awesome veil I was in my early teens and I'd had my tonsils out at our local hospital. Each morning the message went around the ward: 'Matron's coming.' Nurses scurried about, straightening the counterpanes, turning all the bed wheels to face the centre of the ward and clearing away traces of normal activity, like bedpans and tooth-cleaning mugs. Matron, escorted by the ward sister, entered wearing her badge of authority – a magnificent, white, starched veil. She stopped at the end of each bed.

'Good morning, how are you this morning?' she asked. We always said we were doing well. Faced with that veil we wouldn't have dared reel off a list of complaints. How wonderful to command such respect, I thought.

Several years later I got the chance to wear a veil when I worked in a hospital. But ours were made of cardboard. They were flat when you bought them and you slotted the pieces together until they formed the right shape. When they became grubby you just tore them up and threw them in the rubbish bin. No more washing, starching and ironing. But that cardboard wasn't nearly as impressive as the old starched muslin. On my first day at work I pinned on the veil with hair clips and marched off to my ward. A junior nurse saw me coming and opened the ward door. I gave her a gracious smile and swept through. Unfortunately a sudden draught uplifted my veil and it fluttered to the floor. The nurse picked it up and handed it to me. With as much dignity as I could muster I pinned it on again, watched by the amused patients in the first two rooms of the ward.

The mile

Keith Robertson

MY BROTHER AND I had been on the back-country sheep station for barely a couple of months when we first heard about the New Year games. They were a bit like a Caledonian games at which the athletes competed for prize money. The mile was the big event and we whistled when we heard the amount the winner would receive – it was almost a man's wages for a month!

'There are some quite good athletes among the blokes over the river,' said our boss. 'I can't see that we'll still be shearing at New Year and the season's so dry there shouldn't be any urgency about the hay so the pair of you could go to the games if you wanted to.'

'Might be a bit of fun this year,' said Bert, one of the station hands. 'There's a new cowboy just up from the city. The boys over there have had him out training and by keeping just behind him they've kidded him he's a great runner. In fact, they've told him he's so good he should concentrate on the mile.'

My brother and I grinned at each other. As city-bred boys we knew what it was like to be had-on by new chums. We did have some sympathy for the new fellow, but it was all good fun, and besides, we'd never struck this game before.

We occasionally came in contact with the other station's hands over the next two weeks when one or other of us was riding around near the boundary, or we spoke to the rural delivery man or a visiting agent. The news about the young lad spread round the district and became the current joke. I suppose that, in a way, it was a good advertisement for the games – and we decided we'd definitely go.

The New Year's Eve dance was a high-spirited affair and a roaring success. The next day we went to the games. The host township was quite small and we were a little disappointed to find there wasn't a full 440-yards track. However, there was a happy spirit everywhere and people sat about on the embankment and had a good, old-style picnic – a happy family day. As each event passed it became clear that some of the young men were pretty good athletes, in spite of the night before.

Towards mid-afternoon the games reached their highlight – the mile. When the call came for the entrants to gather we sensed a barely restrained mirth around the ground as those in the know pointed out the young cowboy – but there was also genuine excitement as this was the big event. Some of the contestants were beginning to show signs of the night before as well as the effects of enthusiastically taking part in some earlier events. The handicapper stood a few of those known as 'gun' runners on the starting line and then started pacing his way around the track stopping here and there to place the other runners. He put the young cowboy almost halfway around the track. I don't know if there had been some good-natured collusion but what followed suggested it. The cowboy was starting out in front and he'd been told that when the race started he had to run as fast as he possibly could. The pistol cracked and off they went – most of the runners in a measured stride. But the lad took off as if he was running a 100-yard sprint. The pre-race sniggering now broke into open laughter. By the time the back starters had completed their first lap they were level with the cowboy. But of course, he was a lap ahead!

We began to sense a change. The main runners were beginning to show the strain and the crowd began to realise that the cowboy was still ahead with only half a lap to go to the finish line.

Just like Harold Abrahams commentating at the 1936 Berlin Olympics we were all shouting, 'Come on Jack!' At last the lad fell across the line just ahead of the other runners and we went wild. The underdog had come through!

Over the years, I've seen many fine miles, by many fine runners. But to this day, the mile, for me, will always be that one raced so many years ago, in the heat, on that small, dusty country ground by the young cowboy with guts and a strong sense of self-belief.

Me (standing) and the driver Bill Clarke, preparing for the return trip to Motuhora.

Working on the trains

Maurie Moor

I STARTED WORK on the Motuhora line in 1942 as a young locomotive fireman when I was still a single man. I'd come from a big city and the baching, the hills, the tree stumps and the boredom of the place started to get to me, so I decided to marry my fiancée and we were married in February, 1943.

During those war years we didn't have cars so train travel was the thing. The Motuhora to Gisborne line was a busy one in those days. We had two train crews stationed at Motuhora and worked the roster between us – Monday, Wednesday and Friday one week; Tuesday, Thursday and Saturday the next. And a long weekend every other fortnight.

We spent quite a bit of time at the Matawai pub and usually travelled there on the railway's jigger. Luckily, it was downhill on the way home!

As well as a passenger car and guard's van our train pulled wagons of livestock and native timber logs and loads of blue chip-metal from the Motuhora quarry. We took the school children to Te Karaka station and we picked up passengers, and dropped them off, at railway stations, road crossings and farm gates anywhere along the way. The guards even picked up library books and changed them for readers during their two-hour break in Gisborne.

On the return trip the passengers' parcels of fish and chips, or babies' bottles, were taken up to the engine and placed on the boiler to keep warm until their station.

We had our fun and our disasters. I recall one shocking incident when the train was pulling out of the Te Karaka station. Stockmen were working cattle in the railway stockyards when a horse took fright, broke loose and bolted for the road crossing. As the train reached the crossing the fireman looked out his side window in time to see the tail end of the horse just beat the train over the crossing. Then he noticed a doll's pram rolling down the path. At the next station they heard that the line gang had found the body of a ganger's four-year-old daughter. The horse had knocked her onto the track in front of the train, unnoticed by the train's crew. That same little girl had often stood by her gate to wave at the train as it passed by.

Like many others, that train no longer runs. The service at Motuhora was eventually cut to three days a week and then the Motuhora depot was completely closed down.

1955 licence

Fay Morrow

IN 1955 WE lived in Pongaroa, east of Pahiatua. With my friend Betty, I was coaching my sister-in-law Isobel on the road rules so that she could sit her driving test. The day came when she had to go into the county office where the traffic cop was waiting for her. We had taken Isobel in her own car for the test. When she finished she came out all smiles – she'd passed. Then she said, 'Right, come on now, it's your turn!' I was shocked. Betty and Isobel had jacked this up between them, and to top it off, my little Hillman was away being greased. 'Don't worry,' said Betty, 'I've got my Hudson Terraplane which you can use.' It was a dirty big thing, parked sloping forward into the kerb.

When I went into the office I overheard someone say to the cop, 'Take her down the cemetery road and she'll get her licence.' This cemetery road was very narrow and windy and ran along one side of the local river. I doubted if the Terraplane would fit! The cop came out and as I got in I told him I'd never driven this car before. He said that if I drove it like he'd seen me driving the Bedford truck I'd be OK! I was surprised he'd seen me driving the truck, although my husband and his father were bridge builders and Isobel and I sometimes helped them out with the odd driving jobs even though I didn't have my licence.

Off we went. I was scared stiff that I'd shoot forward and hit

someone. The cop took me up and down a road I knew well and on the way back to the office he asked me about the right-hand rule. By the time we got there he'd written out my licence.

Outside the office we laughed nervously about the day. A young boy asked how I'd got on and when I told him I'd passed he said it was his second try and that he'd found the test very hard. That was 45 years ago and I've had a perfect driving record ever since.

A Sunday outing in the 1920s

Jim Dangerfield

AS A YOUNG schoolboy in the early 1920s, I went on the occasional Sunday afternoon outing from Christchurch to Corsair Bay, a small beach on the shore of Lyttelton Harbour. The day began with our mother filling a substantial wicker basket with lunch to feed us active kids. Then we had to get tidy before walking to the street corner to catch the electric tram to the intersection of Colombo Street and Moorhouse Avenue. From there we walked to the railway station where my father bought our tickets, and we walked along the main platform to the port dock from where crowded trains departed at 20-minute intervals. The trains couldn't leave more frequently because of the bottleneck caused by the single-line tunnel that linked the tomato-growing suburb of Heathcote with the seaport of Lyttelton. As soon as one steam-hauled train cleared the tunnel there was another waiting to occupy it and so the tunnel was always smoke-filled, as were the bench-seated carriages of the long trains. The carriages were not lit so we travelled for what seemed an endless time in smoky darkness.

At Lyttelton there was a rush to get on the launch bearing the sign 'Corsair Bay'. Another launch took travellers to Governors Bay at the head of the harbour and a third crossed to Diamond Harbour. Sometimes there wasn't room on the launch on the short run to Corsair Bay so my father would decide to walk the dusty gravel road. My mother would make her displeasure known, and we'd lose out on time to play on the beach, the water journey, the thrill of watching the docking manoeuvres at the small jetty, and the challenge of manfully stepping from ship to shore.

Everyone wanted to return to Christchurch about the same time in the late afternoon so there was no possibility of getting launch transport back to Lyttelton and again we'd take the road to catch a train, then endure that smoke-filled tunnel. The young ones always had to stand in the centre aisle of the long carriage and the train seemed to take ages before it emerged into the fading afternoon sunlight.

We always slept well after our seaside outing, especially when we'd had to walk there!

Clearing stumps

Loris Mathew

AS A PRE-SCHOOLER in the early 1920s I spent a lot of time with my father, Harry Priest. He was a farmer who was breaking in his land about three miles west of Te Aroha. A large part of the property was very wet with close-standing tea-tree hiding the stumpy remains of a long-gone forest destroyed by a huge fire, which explained the remaining stumps beneath the tea-tree, some still deeply embedded in the soil. Dad had cut the tea-tree with a slasher. He carried a whetting stone in his hip pocket and stopped from time to time to touch up the blade. After he'd cleared the area, he dug out the roots and threw them into a heap to be burnt.

Then the hard work began. The remaining stumps had to be removed and drains dug to get rid of the water before the land could be ploughed. I liked to watch as the stumps were removed. Those on or near the surface were dug out, but the more stubborn ones required sterner measures. First Dad dug around a deep stump until he'd hollowed out a cavity beneath it. Next, he tied his handkerchief to the top of a tea-tree stick and pushed it into the ground at a safe distance – to show me where I had to stand. Then he packed a large charge of dynamite into the cavity, shouted to me, 'Fingers in your ears, now!', lit the fuse and ran. I loved to watch the explosion of dirt and swamp wood rise and fall in a great shower. Sometimes, though, an extra-big stump was only loosened but not blown out. Then the Clydesdale, Gee Fan, was brought up to help, and with a chain secured to the stump, he hauled it out. The stumps were thrown into great heaps – higher than a man – left to dry, and then set alight to burn for days.

Later the drains were dug, all by manpower using only a long-handled shovel. Sometimes, possibly until the area became dry enough to work, rushes grew where the tea-tree had been. These had to be grubbed with a very sharp spade before the land could be ploughed and sown in pasture.

One special memory of rush grubbing is of Dad finding a lark's nest in the shelter of a clump of rushes. He showed it to me after exacting a promise that I'd neither touch it nor tell anyone it was there. He left that particular clump for another day.

Duck shooting

John Wilkie

I MUST HAVE been about 10 when I was invited to spend the Easter holidays with my best friend on a farm at Riversdale, Southland, in the 1920s. I had stayed at that farm before and had had a wonderful time. I'd learnt to ride and even squeeze some milk from a cow at milking time. The farmer didn't think he had enough milking cows to install machinery, so the 11 cows were milked morning and night, all by hand. One afternoon my mate and I went for a walk through the paddock, came to the boundary and crossed over onto the neighbour's property. There was a small stream running through this farm and we followed it down through willows. In the willows we discovered a pond with about 40 ducks on it.

On the way back we decided that the next day we'd get the guns – a double-barrelled shotgun and an automatic Winchester rifle and have a shot at those ducks. Once before, we'd taken the guns for rabbit shooting and had managed quite well.

Next day we peered through the willows and, sure enough, the ducks were still there. Being inexperienced, we stepped out and fired without taking a proper aim. What a flutter! Before we could fire again the ducks were gone, except for one that we'd killed – but it was way out in the centre of the pond where we couldn't reach it. Back home we went, with no ducks to show for our efforts.

The next afternoon we could see the neighbouring farmer coming in on horseback. We knew something wasn't right so we climbed up a fir tree and waited! The farmer was shouting in a rage at my friend's father. After he left we climbed down and were given a scolding about our shooting venture.

It turned out that the farmer had been feeding those ducks for some weeks and had arranged for his friends to come over on the opening of the duck-shooting season.

I never heard if those ducks ever did come back – like lambs to the slaughter.

Early cinema experiences

David Speary

NOT LONG AGO I saw Rudall Hayward's 1928 film *Bush Cinderella* at an Auckland film festival. It was interactive theatre, booing the villain, laughing at the comic, fearing for the heroine, and cheering the hero. We came out exhausted and smiling and it reminded me of the last time I'd seen a Rudall Hayward film in a Queen Street cinema about 45 years ago, soon after we had arrived from England.

Dad insisted my brother and I go to a fleapit at the bottom of Queen Street called the Oxford. The film was Rudall Hayward's 1940s talkie version of *Rewi's Last Stand* and my learning about New Zealand's culture started early.

As children in Surrey we had several cinemas within easy bus ride of our home, but in the East Coast Bays on Auckland's North Shore we only had the 555 Cabaret at Browns Bay. Old photos show it was pretty rough compared with what we'd been used to back 'home'. The front rows of seats were wooden forms or old deck chairs. Unintentional humour was often supplied during tense moments in films when old canvas in the deck chairs gave way. A ripping sound, thump, and loud squawk changed the concentration of the audience from the action on the screen to the embarrassed patron picking himself up off the floor and looking for another seat.

Once I'd started secondary school at Rangitoto College I was allowed to go to the pictures on Saturday nights. I often walked the one and a half miles down to Browns Bay from North Cross Corner, but usually the film ended in time to get the 10.20 bus home. If the film was longer it was a toss-up between seeing it through to the end and walking home, or, if the weather was bad, leaving early to catch the bus home. It cost 1/9, almost half my week's pocket money, for a seat near the front and money for the bus and an ice cream. I liked to be choosy, though, and only went when I thought the film was good enough.

Sometimes we were able to go into Auckland to the cinema. Half the adventure was the ferry ride from Bayswater Point where the bus ride ended. To make it financially worthwhile we had to see two films, as the bus fare, at 2/3 each way, plus the ferry fare, was nearly as much as the cinema price of 3/6.

We would get to town in time to see an 11 o'clock session, rush to John Courts, or maybe even Farmers tearooms, for a quick lunch, and then back to a second film at another cinema for the two o'clock session. The films showed at eleven, two, five and eight and there were no coffee bars or takeaway food places then.

One of my memories of the fleapit at Browns Bay was our end of School Certificate exams celebration in 1959. By then the 555 had been refurbished with real cinema seats from a demolished Queen Street theatre. Our gang went on a Thursday night to see *A Tale of Two Cities* with Dirk Bogarde in the dual role. We'd never have gone out on a Thursday night normally because it was in the school week, and as it was a celebration we sat in the expensive seats, at the huge price of 2/3, and spent at least 2/- on sweets or chocolate to share amongst us.

Oh boy! We young sophisticates really knew how to live it up.

Sounds boyhood

Gordon McArthur

I OFTEN PLAYED truant from school and it's not something I'm terribly proud of. However, one of my most productive periods of wagging school in the early 1940s gave me the chance to get to know one of the real characters of the Marlborough Sounds, Charlie Wise, driver of the *Charmaine* – one of the Steel family's service launches at Picton. On Thursday mornings I would leave for school knowing that the lure of the smell of the sea and diesel and the hard-case banter of Charlie was going to be too much for me. When I arrived at the wharf I would tell him all sorts of lies about how I was there with the blessing of my mother. I don't think schooling was very high on Charlie's list of priorities so there really wasn't a problem – and off we'd go.

What a day it always was! We had parcels, newspapers, bread, groceries and the mailbags to deliver right out to the head of Queen Charlotte Sound. Most places had jetties and my job was to leap off the bow and throw the forward line over the protruding pile or small bollard with a half hitch. Charlie and the residents in each small bay would exchange a few friendly insults, we'd wave goodbye and we'd be off to the next bay. The stops I liked most were those where Charlie would nose the *Charmaine* up onto the beach. The unloading was done with a small ladder off the bow. Sometimes we didn't bother with the ladder and would simply toss the stuff directly onto the beach – not so funny if the bread fell a bit short. Any insults on those occasions were in earnest. Charlie drove the boat quite fast, and sometimes when I was at the bow ready to leap off I'd get a friendly punch on my upper arm, just below my shoulder, and be told to 'get cracking or we'll be dropping the stuff in their kitchen!'

With all the calls completed we'd head for home. I'd boil the billy, roll a couple of cigarettes for Charlie, then he'd step away from the wheel with a mug of tea in his hand and tell me, 'See that point to starboard? Steer for that.' As it got darker it might be, 'See that light to port? Steer for that.' Then he'd tell me stories about his life, which made me smile inside but you didn't laugh out loud at Charlie.

I returned to Picton when I was in my twenties and wandered down to the wharf. I saw the unmistakable bow wave of the *Charmaine* approaching. She stopped, the side hatch door slid open and Charlie Wise stepped out onto the wharf. It was then that I experienced one of the warmest moments of my life. He recognised me and said, 'G'day.' I said, 'Hello Charlie.' Then he asked, 'How ya doin'?' I replied, 'I'm doing OK thanks, Charlie.'

I saw what passed for a smile come over Charlie's face. He punched me lightly on the upper arm, just below the shoulder, and said, 'That's good.' I never saw him again.

New chums on the Limited Express

Barbara Knight

IN APRIL 1957, my husband and I disembarked at Wellington from the immigrant ship *Captain Cook* after six weeks at sea. Several hundred of us, mostly in our mid-twenties, were taken by bus to Wellington railway station to catch the train to Auckland. We'd arrived that morning to start our new lives in our chosen country. We were rather like tourists, eyes darting everywhere, trying to absorb every detail of this strange new place, but unlike tourists we were apprehensive at what was ahead of us. We'd been briefed aboard the ship by Department of Labour officers about an overnight train to Auckland and were given small white tickets to exchange for an evening meal. This was just as well because we'd been at sea for six weeks and no one had funds, or ready cash, left!

We were shepherded into second-class carriages with their hard, upright seats, four to a seat, with a table in between. On the platform we'd seen some people getting pillows – too late we realised why! There was no leg room for the long-legged or our worldly possessions, or, indeed, any room to stretch out at all. But we were young, excited and going on yet another adventure. The train departed about 3.30 and once again our eyes and ears were on full alert taking in all the new sights and sounds. The first place-name was Paekakariki and many were the shouts of laughter as we raw poms tried to pronounce it. We watched the red roofs and white timber walls of the houses sail past. Each stood alone with its own huge garden. Most if us were children during the Second World War with memories of burned-out houses, food and clothing rationing and cramped living conditions. It looked like paradise from that train window. There were many tears of pure relief.

We stopped at Taihape about seven in the evening, only to find that our meal tickets weren't accepted there. We slumped together and eventually dozed off but we were brought back to reality some time later as the train squealed to a stop. A guard shouted out an unintelligible name – which we now know was Taumarunui – and words that we interpreted as 'meal stop'. After a minute or two it dawned on us that we had to get off the train for this. We could see long queues, mainly male, being handed something to eat. Our menfolk joined them, and after quite a while my husband came back with a meat pie and a very thick cup with very strong tea in it. He hurried back to get his own, but he'd been gone only a couple of minutes when the train began to move! Many men moved faster in the next couple of minutes than they'd moved for a good long time and they all managed to scramble aboard the last carriage and rejoin us.

At dawn we stopped somewhere. Department of Labour officers boarded and worked their way through the train. They gave us instructions about our accommodation and when we were to start our new designated jobs. My husband had been a policeman in London and was informed at 5.30 that morning that he would have to reapply to join the New Zealand police within 48 hours of arrival. (Until then he was classified on our travel documents as 'unskilled labourer'!) We were fortunate because we had a sponsor, someone who would guarantee us a roof over our heads and would care for us until we were established, so we didn't have to go to the camp at Mangere. At Auckland station we were met by the elderly lady who was our sponsor and our new life was about to begin.

Three years later we had our second encounter with that overnight express train. We were at the station waiting to collect my husband's parents and sister and we had our two-year-old Kiwi son with us. He was to see his grandparents and aunt for the first time.

What a difference! There we were, after only three years, the proud owners of a house and a quarter-acre section in Avondale, with our own car and all three of us tanned, healthy and well groomed. Suddenly the Tannoy speakers throughout the station began to relay the radio news – a race commentary from the Rome Olympics. Snell had just won gold for New Zealand! 'That's one for Halberg and now one for Snell!'

The whole station erupted into cheers, with us cheering as loud as anyone. As our bemused family got off the train, weary and apprehensive, they saw their Kiwi family dancing up and down with joy. Not at their arrival, as they might have expected, but because some chap had won a gold medal at the Olympics for New Zealand. My mother-in-law confessed many years later that she thought we'd all gone 'troppo' that day.

Mind you, it wasn't long before she could name every member of the All Blacks and the New Zealand cricket team!

Farm holiday, 1912

Gwen Caton

MY FIRST DEPARTURE from familiar surroundings was before the First World War when I must have been about seven years old. Cars were a rarity and bicycles and horse-drawn vehicles were the usual thing – used by doctors who visited the sick, and rural folk when they did their shopping. Walking to school, to visit friends or attend church was the accepted way. This meant that we had a fairly static community where each member was almost as familiar as one's own family. Families were bigger; many having 10 or 12 children, and those children in turn had two or three children more than families do today, so each child had numerous aunts, uncles and cousins. My older brother and I were rich in such relatives. Our parents were both from an eight-children home and cousins abounded in all age groups.

It was quite extraordinary when, as a result of ill health, one of the uncles had taken his doctor's advice and bought a farm in another district. To our family in Kaikoura, the Rai Valley, in Nelson province, was the other end of the earth. Excitement ran high when it was suggested that our families paid a visit to the new farm during the Christmas school holidays. I don't remember any of the preparations but I do remember the day we left. My father wasn't coming, but with us came my aunt and three cousins – two girls and their young, pre-school brother who was always addressed by a Scottish great-aunt as 'wee Wullie'. We had at least two horses and a fairly large carriage because we all went in it, and it was all very comfortable during the three-day journey.

We were excited and gloriously happy, singing and laughing as we left Kaikoura. We looked back at the little bay, with its limestone cliffs, the peninsula pushing out into the sea and the high mountains of the Kaikoura ranges still carrying snow on their peaks. We eagerly looked ahead along the white limestone road towards the great unknown. Each time we passed a well-established sheep station with its homestead and beautiful gardens 'wee Wullie' would ask, 'Is that our sarm?' (His 'f's were 's's at that stage!)

We played 'I Spy', then guessed what we'd see around the next bend, and we counted rabbits that crossed the road in front of us, but there were too many to keep a running total in our minds so we chose a colour and counted only rabbits of that colour. At night we slept like babies in the accommodation house beds and were always ready for another thrilling day.

On the last day we were very excited and finally, there before our eyes, stood an unlined, wooden hut with a corrugated-iron chimney, knee-high grass and a tent nearby for the guests.

'What a sunny sarm' said wee Wullie – a comment echoed in our hearts. Inwardly we children were delighted, although I don't know what the women's thoughts were.

How we loved those hot sunny days, swimming in the creek, riding the sledge, exploring the virgin bush, climbing tree stumps and tickling the trout, which we later ate. Wild pork and venison were new sensations to our palates – and we got to sleep in a tent! From daybreak to dark, life was an untold joy. A shortage of bread one day led to my mother losing her reputation as a first-class bread maker. The flour had gone musty, the wood for the open fire was slightly green, and a camp oven presented an unknown hazard. Mother did her best but the result was a disaster and those sad little loaves from the camp oven became footballs and were passed around, kicked and otherwise misused until they disintegrated and were finished off by the birds. For bread we now had to go to a distant store which was the country type, with everything you needed from axes to candles, bacon and hams in muslin tights to hang from the rafters, and boiled sweets in paper cones. The *Weekly News* and the *Free Lance* were quickly scooped up by the news-hungry customers.

I can't remember anything of the return journey – only the reunion with my father and the tales we had to tell about wee Wullie's 'sunny sarm'. I did not revisit the farm, even after a comfortable home and a garden had been established, so the memory of that first visit remains vivid.

The *Hood* and bananas

Beryl Burgess

IN 1924 OUR headmaster ('The Boss') announced at assembly that he
and a lady helper would be escorting a party to Wellington to see the
two battleships, *Hood* and *Repulse*. I was only 10 years old and hadn't
even heard of these great ships but I smelled adventure and wanted to
join the party. With a promise to 'be good for the rest of my life' I finally
won Dad over and got his permission to go. The great day arrived and
early that morning the 29 people in our party boarded the train for
Wellington. There were no separate padded seats, just one long, hard,
wooden seat down each side of the second-class carriage. We each had
our cut lunch and I was also clutching one shilling for spending money
tied into the corner of my hanky. The journey seemed endless but we
did arrive at the old Wellington railway station, and even the walk to
the wharf seemed to take hours. Then, there it was! The *Hood*, huge and
painted a very dark grey. To get on board we had to experience the
delicious horror of walking over a small bridge while trying not to look
at the water far below – but we couldn't resist a quick peek. We were
split into groups and escorted by sailors over what seemed like acres of
deck, examining huge guns, and up and down narrow, steep stairs into
bunkrooms and engine rooms. On and on we plodded before finally
being rewarded with a drink and a bun.

Then it was time to leave, over the little bridge again, and we headed for the train. I was still clutching my shilling and I was determined to spend it. But where? Luck was with me. We passed a fruit stall and I bought 13 rather ripe bananas and hurried on. Unfortunately I stumbled and fell, badly grazing both knees. The brown paper bag split and the bananas joined me on the ground. The lady helper tore my hanky in half and bandaged my knees, and I gathered up the bananas in the skirt of my best white dress. When we were all safely on the train 'The Boss' saw my sorry state and lifted me and my fruit up into the luggage rack where I immediately went into a deep sleep. Hours later I was woken by my Dad who gently lifted me down and took me home to Mum. She had a large enamel bowl of warm water from the tap on the old kitchen stove, with a liberal addition of cloudy Jeyes fluid, and gently removed the stuck bandages. I had some warm cocoa and a sandwich, then went to bed. We then had a week of bananas and custard, bananas and jelly and banana sandwiches and fritters!

I never forgot the *Hood* but I've always associated it with bananas!

Jimmy and the dictionary

Janet Dellow

AS A YOUNG girl in the 1940s I lived in Timaru. Every Wednesday Jimmy the Chinese greengrocer called at our house and my mother selected the vegetables she wanted. Jimmy would stand on the deck of his small truck and weigh the produce on his scales. They were old scales with the big round clock-like face and a spring hook to the tray. Jimmy would then come inside for a cup of tea, served in our best room, which was used only for special occasions. It was during the latter part of the war I can remember my father advising Jimmy to fly a Union Jack outside his house at Saltwater Creek. This was to show that Jimmy was 'on our side'.

When the big floods of the late 1940s hit Jimmy's market garden he stayed with us for about four days, and it was fun being allowed to listen to the adults' conversations. Later my father helped Jimmy to bring his wife, son and daughter from China to New Zealand. Jimmy called his daughter Janet to show his gratitude – much to my delight.

Janet sometimes accompanied Jimmy on his rounds and we played outside in our backyard. Language was no barrier and I have happy memories of the Chinese Janet entering into the spirit of our games with enthusiasm. However, I also remember Jimmy for a very different reason. One day I was looking up the spelling of a word in a dictionary

'The culprit', aged 8.

for my homework and I came across the word 'bitch'. It leapt out of the page and I could hardly believe my eyes. What a discovery for an eight-year-old! I was quite sure I was the only person in Timaru to know this amazing fact. I was dying to tell someone – but who? My parents were very strict and I knew they would not be impressed. Then I knew. Jimmy would be interested, for sure. With mounting excitement I hurried to our best room where Jimmy was sitting, all by himself, waiting for his cup of tea. 'Jimmy,' I burst out, 'do you know that bitch is in the dictionary and it means a she dog?' Hardly had the words left my lips when in sailed my parents bearing the afternoon tea. I was ordered from the room and with great trepidation spent the next 20 minutes contemplating my fate. It was very hard to concentrate on my homework and I almost wished I hadn't made the famous discovery. Finally, Jimmy left and I heard my parents' footsteps approaching my bedroom.

'Why did you ask Jimmy if he knew what that word meant?' demanded my father.

'Er . . . umm . . . I thought he would be interested,' I replied in a very shaky voice. With that my parents turned and left the room. And that was that. Nothing more was ever said, so perhaps they saw the funny side after all. I will never know.

Getting the message through

Glenys Froggatt

'ONE SMALL STEP for man, one giant leap for mankind,' spluttered the radio. Man had landed on the moon. It was 1969 and my generation could only wonder at how our world had changed.

'Number, please,' said a distant voice, as we cranked the handle on the old black phone attached to the wall. No, we were not putting through a call to a distant call centre but through to the local telephone exchange about a kilometre down the road where, if we were lucky, cousin Des might be on duty. How did he remember which line to connect with which plug on that switchboard? Working on a switchboard for the Post and Telegraph Department required study and passing many exams. Morse code had to be learned as it was essential for the party lines, which each rural village had. We were lucky to have a private line but there was no privacy with the party lines. Anyone with the same base number could lift the handset and eavesdrop on conversations. Most people respected their neighbours' privacy but we all knew which lines were prone to eavesdropping by gossipy neighbours.

Sometimes Des invited us into the back room of the post office. How complicated it all seemed. That switchboard now sits in the Norsewood Museum, a bulky, cumbersome object full of black wires and plugs. The switchboard operator was responsible for alerting the fire brigade in times of crisis and Des recalled how one night he was dozing in his seat in front of the switchboard. It had been a long day. It was coming up to shutdown time at midnight and in rural New Zealand farmers retired to bed about nine so there was little phone activity. Suddenly Des was brought back to earth as the switchboard activated. 'My house is on fire – quick!' shouted a voice and the phone was slammed down. But whose house was on fire? Des was faced with the dilemma of tracking down the nameless caller – and the call had come from the longest party line in the district. Time was of the essence, but by a sheer fluke he managed to associate the voice with a name and rang back to check that he had the correct house. For his efforts he received an earful of abuse for not being quick enough in summoning the fire brigade! Des then had to race outside, break the glass on the fire alarm hanging on a telegraph pole and push the button. Volunteer firemen then had to be rung and told the exact location of the emergency. It was a long night.

Telegrams were a means of communication between various towns but were used only on urgent occasions as they were expensive. Telegrams were submitted in Morse code from one switchboard operator to the next, who then typed up the message on a yellow form before it was dispatched to the addressee. A telegram was inclined to make one's stomach churn. Who had died? It wasn't unusual for the delivery person to wait while the envelope was opened just in case some moral support was required.

Letters remained our main source of communication. The mail was delivered in the mail car, or was slipped into our box by the school bus driver, who covered both jobs. Village residents called at the post office for their mail, which was sorted alphabetically into pigeonholes behind the main counter. A letter or parcel to England took six weeks by boat. After the war, even well into the 1950s, food rationing was still a part of English life and each October Dad would package up food parcels for friends and relatives at 'Home'.

The goods were parcelled up in corrugated cardboard and shredded newspaper, then stitched with a big sack needle into tightly fitting hessian bags lined with calico. Dried fruits, condensed milk, milk powder and chocolate were all regarded as treats.

Elections were a great radio event. The local newspapers always published a list of candidates for each polling area and on the night we huddled round the table writing in the number of votes each candidate received as they were broadcast. We enjoyed maths on these occasions as we raced to work out the winning candidate's majority. How smart we were being able to add up four columns of numbers!

In Grandfather's day all the men gathered outside the post office and as the switchboard operator received the results he'd rush outside and chalk them up on a blackboard. It was a strictly male event. Women were not supposed to be interested in politics.

Office boy, 1928

Norman Newbold

ON GUY FAWKE'S Day 1928 I started work as the office boy in the Auckland Farmers' Freezing Company head office in Endean's Buildings at the foot of Queen Street. I wore the trousers from my father's one and only suit, my school shirt and well-polished school boots. My main job was to deliver shipping documents, tallies, load-out programmes, and various papers to the vessels at the wharves and to the shipping company offices. Another task was to go out and buy staff lunches. I wasn't allowed to start collecting the orders and the money before 11.45. Sandwiches were a penny ha'penny, buttered buns a penny, pies threepence, Hellaby's pork pies fourpence, cakes a penny ha'penny, fly cemeteries tuppence. I generally managed to get back in time to deliver to the lunchroom by midday except when some individual ordered six penn'orth of fish and chips – a feast. I had to go up to Customs Street for that.

The staff could buy a carcass of reject lamb for fourpence a pound and a side of reject pork for sixpence a pound. You could have the pork delivered to the Hydra Bacon Company at the top of College Hill and have it cured into bacon and ham for a penny ha'penny a pound. It was properly cured, too – in the salt stack for six weeks then taken out and washed and then hung up in the smokehouse. When anyone ordered lamb, that became my problem. The lamb was delivered to the Kings'

Wharf local storage freezing chambers as a frozen carcass. When anyone wanted a piece of their lamb it was my job to saw off what was wanted. All I had was an ancient carpenter's saw that hadn't been sharpened for years. With no rail to hang the carcass on, the only way to attack it was to stand it on its neck on the floor and steady it against anything stored in the chamber, holding on with one hand and sawing with the other – a slow job. My hands quickly froze and sometimes, after a couple of days, the skin would peel off my fingers. The floor in the storage chamber was far from clean, so when I'd finished with it the carcass showed plenty of signs of contact with the floor where it had slipped out of my grasp and fallen.

One day the entire office staff was assembled in the boardroom and the secretary, A. G. Brown, told us that Prime Minister Gordon Coates had decided that every employee in the country had to have his wages cut by 10 percent, starting from the next day, which was pay day, even though we were supposed to get a week's notice. My wage was cut from 20 shillings a week to 15 shillings. I respectfully pointed out to the accountant that someone's arithmetic wasn't as it should be but I was told that I was still getting twice as much as those poor unfortunates on government relief work.

Eventually I had the pleasure of teaching a new office boy and I was given a position at the end of a long desk in the office. My hours of work were from 9 am to 5 pm, but you were expected to do overtime up to 9 pm without extra pay. However, you did get one shilling and threepence for tea money. With the one shilling and threepence tea money you could have a good three-course meal at Cooke's Restaurant just up from the corner of Customs Street and Queen Street or you could have four half handles of beer and a threepenny pie. Everyone had to be at his desk with pen ready at 9 am sharp. We simply had to conform because there were hundreds desperately wanting work. Actually, there was little or no work done at night. You paced yourself during the day so you didn't have much, or anything, to do at night. None of the heads ever visited the office at night and if they had they would have found most of the staff playing penny poker in the lunchroom and the rest either watching them or gazing out the window at the people in the street or at the boats loading at the wharf.

When Labour took power compulsory unionism was introduced and every large office was asked to send delegates to Wellington to thrash out union awards with the employers' representatives. We were to be in the Freezing Works Clerical Union and our head office sent three delegates chosen by the bosses – not by the staff. Naturally they had instructions to keep wages as they were and to agree to free overtime. Fortunately, there were many other delegates from other firms so that eventually we all had a rise in wages and the free overtime was restricted to four hours a week.

My pay had just about doubled, which meant, eventually, I could actually afford to get married.

School holidays in the early 1930s

Pat Ridding

IN THE EARLY 1930s I was an only child in Wellington and eagerly looked forward to school holiday visits from my New Plymouth cousin Peter. I lived in the centre of Wellington so there were many interesting places within walking distance. We started off with a day's fishing on the wharves. I can't remember if we caught anything but we certainly discovered the fascination of the big ships. We watched with awe as their cargoes were unloaded, swinging perilously in large rope baskets and landing with a thump on the wharf. How we dreamed of sailing on these fascinating, mysterious wonders.

After dinner we were back on the wharves again, this time with my dad, to see the departure of the *Arahura* or *Matangi* on their nightly trip to Nelson. Often we waited for quarter of an hour to watch the departure of the Lyttelton ferry – a larger, faster ship that would race the *Arahura* to the heads.

Another day we walked along Courtenay Place to Rowell's Bakery. I went to Clyde Quay School with the bakery boss's son so we were allowed to spend time in the bakehouse watching huge beaters mixing vast amounts of dough into luscious cakes, bread and scones. We watched the cakes being iced or filled with cream and if we were lucky we were allowed to choose a cake – my favourite was a fly cemetery, filled with fruit and enclosed in flaky pastry. I can taste it even now!

A walk up Tory Street took us to the milk treatment plant. A polite request and a smile gave us access to the stables where the horses that did the milk rounds were kept. They were friends to all the children on their rounds and their droppings were quickly scooped up by keen gardeners.

On our way home down Taranaki Street we walked quickly past Haining Street. I had been warned that mysterious Chinese men lived there in pakapoo dens.

Another treat was the ride on a double-decker tram to Island Bay. We had to wait until the rush hour at five o'clock for this and were very disappointed if someone had taken our front seat up top. We wound our way through busy streets, the Basin Reserve, Athletic Park and finally a glimpse of the sea at the terminus. A ride on the cable-car then a walk through the Botanical Gardens and the old Bolton Street cemetery was another favourite outing. On the cable-car we always sat on the slippery wooden seats outside and, greatly daring, we stretched our legs out and touched the tunnel wall as we climbed up the hill.

On Saturday we went to the 'flicks'. With threepence for admission and a penny to spend I wouldn't have changed places with Princess Elizabeth! We cheered and stamped when Tom Mix vanquished the baddies and 'Our Gang' was another favourite. We loved the unbelievable adventures of the gang and their dog with a black spot around his eye. Once, as a special treat we went with my dad to see his favourites – Marie Dressler and Wallace Beery in *Tugboat Annie*, but our films were much more exciting and we slept though most of that film.

The highlight of all our outings was the day excursion on the Days Bay ferry *Cobar*. We packed our togs, my mother cut our lunches, and off we went, nearly jumping out of our skins with excitement for our day at sea. Sometimes Bert, a family friend from Karori, joined us. Little did I know that he would one day be my husband! The two boys disappeared to explore the ferry while I looked after the lunches and togs. I sat enthralled as we sailed past the old coal hulks moored near the Hutt Road, then across the harbour to Miramar wharf where a large crowd packed on board. Everyone found a place and we were soon tying up at Days Bay wharf. After lunch and a quick swim we all packed back on board for the return trip. All too soon we were back at the ferry wharf and hundreds of happy, sun-drenched travellers made their way home.

The week had passed quickly, but, with the optimism of youth, unmarked by the Depression and the gathering war clouds, we looked forward to our next school holidays.

Surprise lunch

June O'Donnell

WHEN I WAS small I was lucky to have two grandmothers who lived near my school. Grandma, my father's mother, was nearest and I often went there at lunch-time. She ran a very proper house and before I returned to school my face and hands were washed, my hair brushed, my dress pulled down and my socks pulled up. My school reports were read out and all my behaviour remarked on.

Nana was my mother's mother and everything was different at her house. There my young aunts rushed about looking for shoes or cardigans, or polished the large dining room table. They'd bustle and laugh and wave large cloths, which were smeared with yellow polish,

Nana and
'Panka' Grace.

as they kept polishing until they could see their faces in the tabletop. I would look and see mine too. Grandma was thin and ladylike. She wore black skirts, black blouses and a starched white apron. After lunch she'd change the apron for a silk one and move into her sitting room where she sat by the fire to have a sleep. I would never interrupt her.

Nana, on the other hand, never seemed to sit still. Buxom, up to her elbows in suds, she would wash a huge sinkful of dishes, scrub the wooden bench till it was white then hang the washcloth outside on a branch of the pear tree. She'd let me into her huge bedroom where she tidied herself – putting on a pretty dress of navy blue silk with tiny white flowers to be ready for visiting friends. One lunch hour I rushed home from school to Nana's because it was her turn to have me. She sat me down in the kitchen beside the range at a small table set just for me. She was in a hurry. On the range was a large black cauldron full of bubbling soup. It smelled very good.

'Here you are,' she said. 'Eat it up then you'll have to run to school. I made it this morning.'

She placed a big bowl of hot vegetable soup and a plate with bread and butter in front of me. As I ate I noticed some small black dots that reminded me of full stops floating among the flakes of carrot, parsnip, onions and peas. I stopped eating and Nana noticed.

'Don't worry about those,' she exclaimed, 'I put in a handful of birdseed instead of lentils by mistake. They won't hurt you!' That would never happen in Grandma's house, I thought. I said nothing, finished off my soup, kissed Nana and ran back to school wondering all the way if I'd start to chirp!

The return trip

Leone Proctor

IT WAS WARTIME and I was a young Blenheim teacher at a sole-charge school, Woodbank, at Clarence Bridge, about 25 miles north of Kaikoura. At that time the main trunk railway ended at Clarence but trains only ran on weekdays. One Friday I went back to Blenheim to buy a new frock for a patriotic dance to be held at Clarence on the Saturday evening. On Saturday afternoon I got on a train at Blenheim knowing it would take me only as far as Ward which was barely halfway and I planned to hitch-hike from there. Carrying my old hatbox, I set off and, after passing only a couple of telephone poles along the road, a little old farm truck pulled up. The driver was astonished when he heard my destination and generously he offered me a lift as far as Ure Bridge, about eight miles further on. As we trundled along he offered me his bicycle to complete my journey as long as I returned it, by train, on the Monday morning. I promised to do that and collected the bicycle. It had no gears and a wheel-activated dynamo lamp but the weather was kind to me in the early part of the ride and I made good progress on the straight, but soon the route became hilly and the road surface less friendly. It wasn't long before twilight, and then darkness, descended. Of course, the bicycle lamp wouldn't function when my speed decreased going uphill, but it was just adequate when I rode downhill! A head wind got up, bringing with it squally showers and I longed to see the flicker of a cottage light.

Eventually I reached Wharanui homestead and I decided to phone ahead to my landlady at Clarence who might be concerned that I hadn't returned. So I summoned up courage and rode up to the imposing homestead. You can imagine the tousled spectacle that I presented to the lady who answered the door! I explained my predicament and she let me use her phone but there was no reply.

A fresh bout of determination spurred me on so I set off again. There seemed to be hills where there never had been before on that long ride. At last I spied a solitary light on the brow of a hill, which I suspected belonged to an air force radar encampment within a few miles of Clarence. I pedalled full speed ahead on a much better road, round a bend and the flickering lights of the village greeted me. I got to the dance by 10.30 and the bicycle was duly returned on Monday morning.

A dance was not to be missed in the war years!

Waimataitai school march

Doris Spowart

IN 1954 I went straight from teaching in a small Southland district high school to Waimataitai, a Timaru school of over 700 pupils, and I suffered quite a culture shock. Pupils from Standard Two upwards were either in a boys' class or a girls' class.

At the beginning of April, after the end of the swimming season, each teacher arranged pupils according to height, tallest in front, and shortest at the rear. The children were then arranged in fours, and their seating positions were fixed for that year. All the pupils wore uniforms – navy gym frocks, white blouses, black and yellow striped tie for the girls while the boys wore navy shorts, school jerseys and socks with yellow stripes.

The school was renowned for its silver band, which had been started 20 years earlier. The band had about 30 boys and their instruments included cornets, euphoniums, trombones, double bass, bass drums and side drums. Every Thursday morning interval you could hear a wild cacophony of all the instruments being tried out at the top of the infants' playground. The infants swarmed around their heroes in the band like bees around a honey pot, full of admiration for the 'big boys' who played in the band – and the band boys lapped up the adulation.

A feature was the school march. Every Thursday when the school

bell rang to signal the end of interval 500 children from the senior school ran to their assembly point in front of their teacher. The headmaster, Sam Sullivan, blew his whistle, and there was complete silence. 'Boom boom bi boom! Boom boom bi boom!' was belted out on the big bass drum. The whistle blew again. 'School forward – left, right, left, right,' and the march was on its way. Form Two girls led the rest of the girls' classes, then came the band, then the boys led by the Form Two boys. The pupils marched on the road and the teachers walked on the edge of the footpath beside them. Everyone slapped down the left foot with great emphasis, arms were swung and heads held erect. No one dreamed of talking. Little brothers and sisters rode along the footpath on their tricycles and proud mothers and grandparents waved from their gateways as they watched the impressive progress of 'The March'.

The procession had to cross Wai-iti Road, one of the main bus routes into town. Sometimes, if the bus was later than usual, the march would have another appreciative audience of bus travellers. After 10 minutes the long line turned back on itself and eyes flashed as the Form Two girls passed the Form Two boys – no one smiled, but the looks were eloquent. The beat continued, 'left, right, left, right'. The instrumentalists gave their best and the senior school marched back into the playground. Then Sam Sullivan blew his whistle and the band stopped, probably glad to be able to breathe freely again. The children dispersed to their classrooms, and I often heard them comment 'wasn't it good to beat the bus today!'

Years later, whenever I saw a procession of adults marching, and someone had that pronounced slap down of the left foot, I wondered, 'was he an ex-Waimataitai pupil?'

West Coast happenings

Vince Wright

RIGHT AFTER OUR honeymoon my wife and I went to a sole-charge school in a little village by Lake Brunner on the West Coast. Every year the ladies of the village earned extra money picking blackberries. The children were sent off to school and then the ladies, wearing their husbands' oldest clothes, set off in a group. Usually they returned just before I dismissed the pupils for the day, but on one particular day they were a little late and passed the school just as the children were being dismissed. There was a rather large lady lagging somewhat behind the others. A local farmer didn't notice her and, thinking all the ladies were off the road, he proceeded to drive his bull along towards a paddock next to the school. The large lady, sensing something was wrong, looked around, saw the bull coming and panicked. She tried to jump a nearby fence and almost did it, but the seat of her trousers caught in the top strand of barbed wire and the old material, unable to take the strain, parted – completely exposing all, and the children watching collapsed in mirth.

Sometime later my wife, by then over eight months pregnant, had just returned from the tiny store and as we sat drinking a coffee we heard a crackling sound. From our kitchen we saw that the hotel over the road was on fire. We rushed outside to see all the locals watching the fireworks but doing absolutely nothing. Outside our wooden fence was a narrow gauge railway for taking sawn timber from the mill to the main railway, and a jigger with a drum of petrol and oil aboard was parked right next to our wood shed and this shed, full of dry wood, was right beside our back door. While the young people of the village emptied our house, the rest of us sprayed the back of the wood shed with water to try and stop it catching fire. Suddenly the hotel collapsed and the wind changed direction, thus endangering the rest of the village.

We watched the smouldering hotel for the rest of the night but, luckily, there was no further damage.

The law was that to retain a hotel licence you had to have a new drinking space within 24 hours of any closure. Can you imagine a village on the West Coast without a drinking hole? The following day the sawmill closed in the afternoon while the locals got together and built a new structure from donated materials.

The village had its new hotel – just in time.

A doll called Potty

Judy Tanner

I CALLED MY doll Potty. She came to me in 1916 in a box lined with soft pink paper. I was five years old and an unexpected present was the most exciting thing that ever happened to me. Potty was beautiful. Her hair was blond and straight, her eyes brown. Someone had dressed her with loving care. Her singlet was knitted in fine wool, her embroidered gown had a matching bonnet, and her petticoat was muslin with tiny tucks in the skirt edged with lace. She was perfect.

I can only guess where my doll came from. Because of this thing called 'the war' there were lots of money-raising events like concerts, bring-and-buys and raffles, and it's very likely that someone won Potty in a raffle and gave her to me. At some time during these war years I was sent to my uncle's farm where my aunt and uncle were very kind to me, but it was Potty who eased my homesickness. I talked to her and cuddled her at night, and when I went with my aunt to gather cones, or feed the chooks, Potty came too.

When I went home after my enforced holiday I went to school and there I learned all about the war and the big 'flu epidemic that had killed as many people as the war had. That was the reason I'd been sent to the farm – to escape the Germans and the germs!

I loved being with the other five and six-year-olds at school. Suddenly I had lots of friends who told me all sorts of interesting things. My friend Annie had red hair and freckles and was naughty in school but fun in the playground. She didn't like dolls. She had four older brothers, so what chance did a doll have? Annie said her mother was cruel. She whacked them with a fly swat if they didn't do all the jobs lined up for them, but Annie was such a happy, fun-loving child it was hard to believe she had a cruel mother. My other best friend was called Alice who had a treasured rag doll. Alice was quiet and shy and shabby. All her clothes were her sisters' grown-out-of dresses.

School was a place of learning, and so was the playground. One day when I came home my mother asked me, 'How was school today?' I replied, 'Bloody good!' I got such a smack on the bottom I went into shock, into tears, and into the bedroom. I told Potty about my terrible mother, and the next day at school I told Annie my mother was a 'bloody bitch'. I felt better after that. I hadn't been at school long before I realised how little my parents knew. In the playground I heard so many strange tales and so many equally strange words. I wanted explanations and answers but all I got was: 'Wherever did you hear that? It doesn't concern you. You're too young to understand.' They just didn't seem to know anything.

When I was nine we moved to a bigger two-storey house. There were so many bedrooms Potty could have had one for herself, but she preferred to stay with me. We had lots of room, lots of land and lots of animals. The animals had to be fed, the cream churned and coal buckets filled. I had to go further to school, had more homework, and piano lessons. I was so busy that, at times, I forgot about Potty.

Sometimes at the weekend, when I was doing childish things like playing mothers and squabbling with my sister, Potty became important again. On one of these occasions my sister broke Potty. It was an accident, but there were tears, trauma and threats. Mother sent Potty to the dolls' hospital. Potty came back with a tear in her eye where a drop of glue had been left. Her face was scarred and her hair matted. This was no longer Potty, my beloved doll. She was no longer a part of my life, and anyway I was nearly a teenager and too old for dolls. So I put Potty in a box lined with soft pink paper and stored her with my other treasures.

Any port in a storm

Jack Salmon

I JOINED THE Royal New Zealand Air Force in 1943 and was posted to Omaka, near Blenheim. I was 18 and my greatest wish was to become a fighter pilot. I spent the first couple of months at Omaka learning how to stick a bayonet into an obliging dummy 'enemy soldier', and then I spent another couple of months at New Plymouth and Rotorua where we were divided into various trade groups. I was lucky enough to be selected as an 'airman pilot under training'. I reported to No 1 Elementary Flying School at Taieri airfield. My logbook shows that I experienced my first flight in a Tiger Moth (under the control of my instructor) and that it lasted just 10 minutes. I enjoyed flying and as the weeks went by I became more proficient in aerobatics, low flying, night flying and the nerve-wracking stopping and restarting of the engine in flight.

In August I was sent off on my first solo cross-country exercise to Lawrence then to Balclutha, Taieri Island and back to base. The weather, although cold, was sunny and windless and I was really enjoying the flight. Then, over Lawrence I started to feel like going for a pee! Now, there is absolutely no place to pee in a Tiger Moth. One option is to hang on, which I did, but I was becoming increasingly more desperate as time went on.

By the time I flew over Balclutha I'd reached my limit and began to

Jack Salmon, airman pilot under training.

search frantically through the many and copious pockets of my flying suit for a possible container. You may remember the tiny bottles that aspirin came in, well, believe it or not, I had the good luck to find an empty one. I filled it and threw the contents over the side. Naturally, the slipstream just blew it all straight back into my face! Meanwhile, my overflow was running onto the floor of the cockpit, so I just gave up and let it go.

When I landed back at Taieri my instructor was waiting to see how I'd got on. He came up to the plane while I was undoing my straps, looked into the cockpit and grinned hugely. Then, without a word, he turned and walked away.

A 1940s Christmas

Dawn Sheppard

IN THE 1940s we had a wartime Christmas on a farm in the Catlins bush in South Otago. Patricia, my niece, was living with us while her mother recovered from an illness. Patricia was six and I was ten. Christmas was that magic, long-awaited time. Firstly, the presents. Patricia's mother had sent a very large parcel all the way from Wellington. I knew because I'd had to collect the mail from the little country post office two miles away. Mum hid the parcel, but when she was out of the house for a couple of hours in the morning and afternoon milking cows, we searched until we found it. It was in a bedroom cabinet, a common piece of furniture from our grandparents' time, which featured an ornate pitcher and bowl on top and a chamber pot in the little discreet cupboard underneath.

We carefully undid the parcel, examined every article and then carefully did it up again. This pre-Christmas titillation was repeated several times and I'm sure Mum must have known. Then we innocent, wide-eyed little girls would subject her to good-natured guessing games about the parcel's contents, asking leading questions about size, shape, colour and quantity. She played along, never giving anything away.

We loved opening our gifts on Christmas Day. In those days our presents were put in a pillowslip left hanging on the end of the bed. I used to re-wrap my presents and re-pack my pillowcase for about a week after the big day so that I could repeat that delight of Christmas morning until at least New Year.

Christmas dinner was another important ritual. Our poultry had to be raised, fed, killed, prepared and stuffed, then put into the wood-burning range to be roasted. That Christmas it was a goose and we two girls, plus the Harris boys from down the road, were given the job of plucking it. We were sent away from the house up to the big stand of macrocarpa trees, which had been planted to shade the original, punga homestead of the pioneering days. What a tedious job it was de-feathering that bird! We dithered and played and stuffed feathers down each other's necks, swung on the branches and threw little seed cones at each other. Then I was called to go and fetch the mail. What a relief! That could take at least two hours if I could spin out the journey over the metalled road, and the plucking would be finished when I got back. When I eventually returned the poor bedraggled bird was hanging in the wash-house, an unappetising lump with a long dangling, bloody neck and feathers still in place over great areas of its mutilated carcass. But Patricia was gleefully triumphant, 'We've done our share. We've left your bit to do!' My bit, of course, was the rear end, and Mum then had to make that sad piece of poultry respectable enough to eat.

The steamed pudding was another part of the big midday meal. It had been boiled in a cloth and then hung out on the clothesline to dry before being put away in a cool, dry safe to 'mature'. There had to be money in it, shining threepences and sixpences, two one shilling pieces and one florin – glittering prizes greatly valued by us children. Patricia hated heavy steamed puddings and usually wouldn't eat them but the chance of financial gain made her doggedly eat on – even to a second or third helping. Her bobbing curls, determined expression and spoon held in an excavating grip are still clear in my memory. So is the exultant yell as the six-year-old struck metal, 'I've bloody well got one!' Mum and Dad laughed until they had to wipe away tears. Another piece of family lore was imprinted in our memories.

Irene's mother, Mrs Bartley, carrying in the firewood.

Day of rest

Irene Bronlund

SUNDAY WAS SUPPOSED to be a day of rest but my mother wouldn't have known it. The Sabbath saw her working almost harder than normal, and wartime didn't make it any easier. She'd be up at dawn on Sunday morning setting the dough for our Sunday treat of yeast buns and organising the midday hot meal. Our special Sunday-best clothes had been ironed, and shoes polished the night before. When she'd got the four youngest dressed for church, and had scrambled into her own Sunday best we'd all dash breathlessly to catch the 7 am bus to our church of the moment – we tended to change every now and then. When we were Anglican we weren't allowed to have breakfast before Communion and our empty stomachs would start to gurgle and we would giggle at the noise. The teeniest sip of wine and something that melted on the tongue was all we got before we returned home at half past nine. After a good breakfast we'd get the hurry-up from Dad to do the farm chores – milk the cows, feed the hens and put the horses out from the stable.

Dad rarely came on these church trips – he was just the instigator. His excuse was the shift work he was on during the war years, or urgent work on the farm.

When we returned from our chores, Mum had stirred and stoked the wood stove and it was ready to receive the Sunday roast. Out came onions, kumara and potatoes to be peeled, beans to be shredded and peas podded. These were our tasks. Mum would baste the roast then she'd get the dough out onto the floured board and knead it into those delicious sultana buns for afternoon tea. While they were set to rise, out came the cooking basin to whip up a Yorkshire pudding to dish up with the roast. Custard simmered on the hob as we poured the peaches from their bottle into the glass dish and carried in the jelly set overnight in the outside laundry.

The man of the house was settled into the sitting room by now, listening to the church service or the news on the radio. Then the table had to be set – starched white linen tablecloth, salt and pepper, a dish of butter with a butter knife and a plate of bread. Knives, forks and spoons had to be laid absolutely symmetrically.

Mum would take off her apron, quickly tidy any wisps of hair and check that the children had washed their hands and done their hair and, as 12 o'clock chimed, Dad rose from his armchair and strode to the table. We'd hold our breath to see what we'd forgotten to do. Dad always said grace and then questioned us on the sermon, which we probably hadn't heard above the rumblings of our stomachs. But Mum gave a report on the sermon and, depending on the mood he was in, Dad continued with a lecture.

On this day of rest Mum still had those yeast buns to cook and inevitably there were visitors for afternoon tea – her fame as a baker had spread far and wide. We had to be quick to get any ourselves! Our bickering over clearing the table and washing dishes wasn't as loud or prolonged as usual and, anyway, Dad was listening. With a bit of luck

Mum might get a few minutes' rest until our return from Sunday school or the arrival of visitors. If the visitors included children, and it was fine, we were sent outside. We'd show them round our small farm and introduce them to the new piglets or to tree climbing, even though we were all in our Sunday best. Sometimes, we would lead them to our bedrooms where we played cards. My eldest sister was certain we'd be struck by lightning for being so wicked.

Mum, meanwhile, was busy getting afternoon tea. After the visitors had gone, and the evening chores done, there was more food – Sunday tea, which was a light meal of bread, buns and cake.

A day of rest? Of course it was. On Monday the real work began – washing day with coppers to light, tubs to fill, and lines and lines of clothes to be hand-wrung, hung up, propped and dried. The six days of labour had begun again.

Milking

Jim Henery

JUST BEFORE THE Christmas holidays in 1931 my parents made a sudden decision to visit my sister in Rotorua. Then my mother remembered the cow and asked who would milk it while she was away? During our younger days we had had up to three cows providing plenty of milk, butter and cream, but by this time we were down to one cow and my mother always did the milking. I had no great love for these animals and I was a reluctant cowboy, not very happy about having to tend them, cut extra grass from nearby paddocks and separate the milk, but one look at my mother's face and I bravely stepped into the breach and volunteered to do the milking. 'What?' exclaimed my mother, 'You've never milked a cow in your life!'

I defended my hasty decision and reminded her that I'd often watched her milking and so she accepted my offer with some misgiving. There was no opportunity to test my ability to do the task before she left for Rotorua, so on the evening of my parents' departure I followed what she always did and passed the bucket through the gate leading to the cow bail, while the cow waited patiently outside. As a friendly gesture I copied my mother's habit of placing a reassuring hand on the cow's rump. She was then supposed to walk into the stall.

But not this time: she turned her head towards me and with a scornful look took off down the paddock. I trailed her round that paddock, through the gate into the next one and finally back to the bail entrance. No sooner had she got there than she took off again. I must have tried at least six times to get her in. I finally gave up and called out in disgust, 'You can bloody well milk yourself then!'

Next night I tried again. When I placed my hand on her rump she just walked quietly into the bail. I locked the headstall and tied the leg rope and I had no problems milking her. After I released her she wandered off back down the paddock.

'Right, old girl,' I said. 'We have a deal. We'll milk every *second* night!'

Motorbiking adventure

Dorothy Black

FOXTON WAS ONCE an important shipping port for Manawatu, and coal, landed from Greymouth, was stored there for use by the railways. It was also an outlet for the larger Manawatu agricultural area where some of my relatives lived, and where we often spent our holidays when I was young – so we knew it well.

My father was a dedicated bikie. Not the black-leathered variety, but a tradesman who was proud to own a motorbike at a time when only New Zealand's well-to-do could afford a car. I don't know what kind it was. I was too young to be interested except to know it took our family up north to visit our much-loved cousins. Mother sat in a handsome sidecar, built by my father, with my small brother on a fixed mushroom-like stool in front of her. He could just peer over the top of the sidecar's polished sides and I was perched crossways on a little seat behind my father. More often than not I'd get the stitch as we bounced up and down over the potholes and corrugations of the metal main road. I've never forgotten how painful that could be.

On Saturdays during the winter my father with his brother and mates would congregate on the back steps of our house at the top of Tinakori Road in Wellington and pull their treasured bikes to bits, oiling and fussing over them in preparation for an approaching holiday.

Dorothy with her father George
Maslen and brother Georgie, 1920.

When the big day came we'd head north over the Paekakariki 'goat
track', then up the coast through Waikanae, Otaki, Levin and Shannon.
In summer these trips usually went well with only the occasional
mishap or breakdown. At those times we would sit by the wayside while
Dad fixed things and Mother found it all very amusing. In winter it
could often be a different story.

On one trip, a bad storm had hit the coastal area and the rivers were
raging torrents, flooding the flats on their way to the sea. Crossing the
low-lying bridges was hazardous as water swirled angrily around. There
were no road lights so it was very dark and the rain was heavy and
chilling. At one river we found the southbound traffic backed up where
a bridge had been swept away. A makeshift affair had been rigged and
worried men were trying to shepherd the travellers across safely.

Mother, my brother and I were carried over, and my father was left to cross under the direction of the men flashing torches and shouting advice. I was very sure both my father and our bike would disappear into the depths below. But, no, he made it and we were all thankful to get home safely.

Those were certainly the days of adventurous travel, and although I'm not sure of all the words, this is the little ditty my mother sang as we bumped along:

O how can we cross the broad river Ohau
O Waikanae not reach the shore.
Otaki a boat and Aroa across
As the Manawatu did before.

What my mother told me

Jewell Dell

AROUND 1930 MY mother gave me some instructions on how I was supposed to behave and I can still remember her words of wisdom. Never go out with a safety pin in your bodice. You might have an accident and then what would the nurse in the hospital think? It is all right to let the lace around the bottom of a petticoat show, but never the material. The same applies to a low-cut décolletage. Only the lace may pop above the bosom of a ball gown. Showing the practical bits of your underwear was not merely forward, it was positively sluttish.

It is lazy to sit and read. You should be embroidering a doily for your glory box. Every girl must have a glory box, whether or not she has immediate intentions with a young man. Every payday you must put money towards a supply of damask table linen, which you'll need when you marry.

Hens only lay well when they have a rooster to run with. That, I think, was a subtle attempt at sex education, a subject which was never mentioned.

Don't pat strange dogs, only stroke them. A pat upsets his nerves and he might bite.

A woman's knees are the ugliest part of her – cover them. Comfortable shoes are not fashionable ones. Only questionable women wear trousers – skirts become ladies. Make-up is bad for your skin.

Always wear a hat outside. Keep your knees together when you sit. When seated on the ground at a picnic sit with your knees to one side and keep your skirt over them. Sitting with your feet out in front of you, toes pointing up, is only for older couples. Keep your back straight at the table by placing a straight stick across your back and under your arms. It is then impossible to reach anything, or hand anything round, and is, therefore, a most effective slimming method. Walk the length of a tennis court on the tips of your toes with your hands crossed behind your back. This assists with good deportment.

Always cream butter and sugar together with your fingers in a china bowl. Fingers are better than a wooden spoon. So said my mother, but it was my gym mistress who told me that horses sweat, men perspire and ladies glow.

Nursing memories

Isabel Campbell

DURING MY NURSING training days in the 1950s there was one very busy day in the baby room. There was no one else to help with all the feeding that day so I propped up some of the easier feeders in the bassinets with their bottles, but in came the ward sister and what a telling off I got! It was overheard by the passing boiler man who stopped me a few days later and said, 'Nurse McKenzie, get married, don't stay here. I remember when that sister came here – the loveliest, fun-loving girl.' To me she appeared a handsome and excellent disciplinarian who insisted that everything be done according to the rules for the benefit of the patients.

In the early days of training the strict discipline was quite awesome. It was usual to enter the ward sister's office in order of seniority – senior nurse, middle, then junior nurses. We then stood to attention with pen and notebook ready to take down the instructions for that day. The ward sister, in all her unquestioned authority, gave out the orders. One day the new middle nurse thought she heard that she was to swab and dress the penis of an elderly gentleman on a traction bed with a fracture. While the embarrassed nurse was trying to do this the patient kept saying, 'What are you trying to do, nurse?' Then someone came along and told her she was supposed to swab and dress the pin ends that held the fractures in place!

Celebrating after first year exam results (Isabel McKenzie, far right).

There was a very strict disciplinarian in one ward. A good teacher, but feared by the students. One day, two friends were on duty together and as one was passing the narrow flower room where we also tested urine samples in test tubes in a rack she thought she saw her friend bending over so gave her a vigorous kick. The one bending over turned around – it was the ward sister. The kicker went into shock, blurting out apologies, but the ward sister closed the matter by saying, 'I take it as a compliment, nurse, that you think my rear view is anything like that of your friend!'

Attention to detail was part of our training and we had a matron who was renowned for pointing out even the smallest imperfection during ward inspection. One day it was my duty to go around, before her inspection, and examine locker tops for cleanliness; bedrails, windowsills, wash-basins and downpipes for dust; to check that bed wheels were in alignment, the curtain pleats straight and the bed quilts crinkle-free. All went well with the inspection until the last room, which had four beds. In my brief absence two frail ladies had got into bed together, the sprightlier one explaining that her friend was lonely!

Night duty was a time when the rest of the world was asleep. The night porter was dozing in his chair one night when the telephone rang and he was ordered upstairs to take a patient to the mortuary. The lift clanged open and he pushed his trolley up to the side of the bed, only to find a cardboard box with a mouse laid out in it! One nurse was heard complaining that she was on her last night duty and hadn't had any emergency obstetric cases. Shortly after the ward phone rang. A voice said that an emergency case had just come in and that she should prepare a bed in a single room. The lift clanged up and she went out to receive her patient. What a sight met her eyes! The patient had rouged cheeks, what looked like a floor mop on her head, wore dark glasses and had a huge stomach. It was the night supervisor in disguise.

In the nurses' home, we were often bothered by men ringing to ask the nurses out. One nurse suggested we should dress up for them. She had an amazing pair of buckteeth made by a dentist friend and another nurse had a red nose attached to a pair of glasses. When the bell rang, the two nurses, dressed in the most outlandish clothes they could find, went out to meet the men. 'Let's get the hell out of here,' said one of the would-be Romeos and they sped off.

Living together in the nurses' home we shared each other's dilemmas and were able to help each other. We had monthly student meetings, dances, garden clubs, class picnics, barbecues, inter-hospital competitions, fundraising events with guest speakers, and film evenings. There was a weekly prayer meeting when we prayed for patients and nurses.

Eventually, it was time to celebrate our state finals. We had a fun party at a crib at Oreti Beach. Partners were invited for an evening of games, surprises and a special supper. Santa arrived, and then the supper. The cakes were decorated to look like kidneys, hearts, livers and other body organs. It was a night of celebration and fun before we assumed rather more dignified roles as registered nurses.

Songs my mother sang

Shirley Schmidli

ALTHOUGH THERE WERE only three of us – my mother, my brother Jack, and I – we were a proper family. Other children had fathers, but ours had died when we were babies and we'd been told he was in heaven and, of course, we were too young to miss him. We may not have had a father but we did have a mother who sang like a nightingale. She made up songs with silly words for us, and when it was bedtime, instead of just saying, 'Off to bed now', she would turn the phrase into a song with trills, arpeggios and coloratura acrobatics. We could never disobey such a charming command. She was our life and our happiness.

She sang for other people too. One year she was the soprano soloist in *The Messiah* at the Dunedin Town Hall. Jack and I didn't know exactly what that meant but we sensed her excitement and tension in the weeks before. We were packed off to bed early every evening and through the wall we could hear her practising, over and over.

Jack and I slept in the same bed, top and tail, and this often caused squabbles. One night I lay awake after Jack had finally fallen asleep. Mother started to sing a tender, haunting aria which I'd never heard before. I was filled with melancholy and started to weep, although I didn't know why. I called out to her and, breaking off her singing, she hurried into the bedroom, looking cross, 'What is the matter?' she

Shirley and Jack.

asked, leaning over me. But I couldn't explain. Hiccupping with distress, the best I could come up with was, 'Jack's touching my feet again.'

Mother looked down sceptically at Jack's still, sleeping form. 'You must be good and let me practise,' she admonished, 'or I'll make a mistake when I sing in the Town Hall. The whole orchestra will have to stop playing and the conductor will be very angry.'

On the night of the performance she came into the bedroom in her yellow velvet evening dress and quickly kissed us goodnight. She seemed to be thinking of something else.

Hours later I was woken by the light from the hall as she opened the door and tiptoed into our room. I smelled her perfume and looked up into her face. Jack sat up, his hair standing up in tufts and we both stared at her.

'Did you go wrong, Mummy?' I asked.

'Not even a little bit,' she cried. She swept us both into her arms, laughing and joyful. What hugs and kisses we had that night. She was ours once again.

Taking the van down the coast

Tom Spence

IN 1958 I gathered up three dogs, a saddle, a bridle, a Ford Thames van, my wife Shirley, two-year-old son Mark and four-year-old daughter Janet. I was leaving the family farm to take up a shepherd's job on Otanga Station at Lottin Point, several miles beyond Hicks Bay.

In the late 1950s it was a three-and-a-half-hour journey from Gisborne to Lottin Point. At Potaka we turned seaward and drove through the bush, through five gateways and two open concrete water crossings, to finally reach the gate at the top of the hill where the wonderful view of Lottin Point and the beach sparkled in the sunlight before us.

We were fortunate to go into a new house overlooking the shore where the pohutukawa trees were in full bloom – a magical place where we spent 12 months, but we will always remember the journeys between the station and Gisborne. The bitumen road ran out a few miles north of Tolaga Bay and from there to Lottin Point it was mud or dust, depending on the season.

At New Year we decided to have a break and go to Tauranga, around the coast, through Opotiki. We made a wooden seat and a bed for the children in the back of the van and everyone was comfortable and happy as we approached Raukokore Bridge. Suddenly, there was a great cracking noise in the back of the van and we were suspended, rear wheels spinning off the ground. We were stuck. A large, loose bridge plank had flipped upwards with such impetus that it cracked through the wooden floor of our smart little van. Thank heavens no one was sleeping just there! There was no one to help us but eventually we got the plank out from under the van and our poor reluctant children were coached back inside with promises of all sorts of good things in Opotiki.

Every three months I made a trip into Gisborne for station supplies. On one of these the station Chevrolet truck was loaded with 45 sacks of potatoes to be sold in Gisborne at 7/6 per bag; 30 sheep skins; four 44-gallon benzine drums to be refilled; a pile of sacks to be refilled with coke for the Aga stove; one washing machine and one vacuum cleaner, both to be repaired; one 20-litre jar to be refilled with formalin for curing foot rot and a large number of empty brown bottles. The truck was standing outside all ready to go at five in the morning, but it rained all night and the engine was wet and wouldn't start. I found the wet part and dried it in the Aga and then we were ready to leave. Our first problem was water across the road by the roadman's cottage at Hoia. It looked all right but we didn't want to take any chances so Shirley waded through in front of us, up to her knees in cold water. After many hours on the road we made it to Gisborne in the late afternoon to unload and leave the truck at H. S. Motors for overnight repairs.

We picked it up at three the next afternoon and loaded it to capacity with the bags of coke, drums of petrol, gate timber, sheep drench and dips, formalin, boxes and boxes of post staples and electric fence insulators, a ton of wire and who knows what else!

The next morning at six we set off on the six-hour trip home. Another successful shopping trip was over!

The bridge

Peter Dawe

IN THE LATE 1940s and early 1950s I was a schoolboy living in Waimate. We didn't own a car but sometimes my grandmother would drive up from Invercargill in her 1936 Morris 8 and for a few weeks, much to our joy, we were able to travel further afield than our bikes would take us.

Our favourite trip was to Oamaru because that meant we had to cross 'The Bridge'. This was the old combined rail and road structure, the best part of a mile long, which crossed the Waitaki River. The railway lines were bolted to the top of the bridge deck and the cars had to straddle the left-hand line, one wheel between the line and the side of the bridge, and the other in the middle of the tracks. The Morris 8 was small enough to fit in the gap without the need to straddle the line so we had no worries about passing oncoming traffic.

The road entrance to the bridge was controlled by a gatekeeper at each end who had to close the gates half an hour before the train was due. The gates were closed and as soon as the last cars were clear of the bridge the signals would be lowered for the oncoming train. After the train had passed the gate would be opened and cars could then cross the bridge again.

In the 1940s there were few problems, but as the 1950s wore on the vehicles began to get wider, and often had a lower chassis, which sometimes struck the metal railway track. The traffic became heavier, too, so planning began for a new bridge. The problems were vividly brought home to me one day when I returned by bus from playing a rugby game in Oamaru. Our bus was about three-quarters of the way along towards the Canterbury end when we literally came up against a large lorry. It was obvious that we couldn't pass each other and it was decided that the lorry would have to reverse. But first, everything behind the lorry had to reverse out of the way. Then the fun started. The lorry was an articulated unit and the driver had only taken delivery of it that morning. You can imagine the scene as the unwieldy monster, with its inexperienced driver, swung first to one side and then the other. Eventually, however, he succeeded in reversing right off the bridge and we were able to continue on our way to Waimate.

A few years later the new bridge was opened and the old road gates closed for the last time. The railway signals were taken down and 'The Bridge' gatemen faded into history.

The chemist's shop

Jewell Dell

I'VE JUST BEEN to the eye specialist and suddenly it brought back memories of the one I visited nearly 70 years ago. Actually, in those days it was more the chemist's shop than the optician. I sat on a chair, swinging my legs, waiting for my appointment and I could see what the chemist was doing. His trouser legs ended in very polished black shoes and his hands were slender and steady, the sort you would have confidence in. I watched them counting and measuring, and weighing out powders and crystals on brass scales which had a small suspended tray for the weights. But mostly I remember his shop. It was never a place to browse in. No one ever said, 'Just looking, thank you.'

It was a dull and dingy workroom by today's standards, a place full of mysterious shadows with dark varnished walls, cabinets and counters. There were two ornate containers made of coloured glass. One was a lovely purple colour and about two feet high, which was the sole display in the tiny front window where it occasionally caught the sun and flashed in the light. There was another greeny-blue one up by the counter and it must have been immensely heavy. Inside the glass-topped counter, in a very small space, were things like razors and razor straps, surgical scissors and items hidden in boxes. The rest of the chemist's stock-in-trade was in heavy wooden drawers, which had been shellacked to a dull brown. These had creamy white labels written on in large and curly letters, which reminded me of school lessons. The drawers slid out to reveal heaps of little blue packets, glass eye-droppers and corks for stopping the bottles, which lived in the adjoining drawers. There were blue eye-baths, cone-shaped medicine measures with little lips like jugs for pouring. Dimpled poison bottles were brown. There was brown, oiled silk, which was put over a poultice to keep in the heat and moisture to 'draw' a wound or sore. The silk was measured off in inches then cut and wrapped in stiff brown paper. There were also loose commodities in those drawers. I recall getting bluestone crystals, which Dad used in our garden; and there was one labelled 'Bis. Mag'. I think it was for indigestion, and you could buy it by the scoop. Flagons of more dangerous stuffs were stored under the dispensing table and there were boxes of larger bottles and jars under the drawers. There were square bottles up on a shelf with powders in them. One was labelled 'Calc. Carb'. Names were never written in full – probably because the writing was so large. Obviously, the chemist knew the shorthand but I thought it was a secret language. Household requirements could be bought at the chemist. Like oxalic acid, which removed ink stains – a necessity at our house!

A great big eye hung outside the chemist's to let you know that the optician was also in that shop. It looked ghastly, much more likely to frighten off the customers than bring them in! The optician, Mr Azzopardi, had a big black leather chair, like a dentist's chair, but not so frightening. The squares and circles, red and green lights used in eye tests haven't changed much, nor have the cards of graduated letters to read. But the spectacle frame into which the lenses slotted was a lot heavier then and really hurt your nose. It certainly left marks on mine. There wasn't much choice in the way of spectacle frames either. They were all the same, horn-rimmed and most unbecoming. No wonder I was called 'four eyes'.

The Nelson train

Jean Williams

I LIVED IN Richmond, Nelson from 1910 to 1918 so the train, which ran through the Waimea Plains and went to Glenhope, was an important part of my life – and in the lives of those who lived anywhere between Nelson and Glenhope. Those fertile plains produced many sheep, cereal crops, hops, fruit and vegetables which were transported by the train, and each day the country boys and girls who attended school or the colleges in Nelson relied on it for transport. I can remember my older brothers and sister dashing down the hill to catch the train to college. There must have been at least two daily trips each way because people from outside the city caught it to go and do business there, and I remember being taken to the city when I was a small child so my mother could do some shopping or visit her friends. When we reached Nelson my mother would take a landau or some other type of carriage to her destination.

Between the steam engine and the carriages were wagons carrying logs, chaff, coal and all sorts of goods. The carriages themselves were of light wooden construction with seats running lengthwise. Later the first-class carriages had padded seats much as we know them today. Right at the back was the guard's van. The engine was coal-fired so the smoke left a fine coating of soot over everything and if the smoke got in your eyes it could bring with it tiny fragments of burnt coal or cinders which were very painful and not easy to remove, but the corner of a handkerchief often did the trick.

The most important train journeys in my life were those to Glenhope to catch the Newman's coach, which ran through the Buller Gorge to Westport. We usually had an early start and went down to the station in our sulky or the gig. It was a long trip because at each station a considerable time was taken up in shunting wagons that had reached their destination and taking up others for stations further down the line. I can remember long waits at each station as the engine took on water from overhead tanks and the ritual of a railway man who went along the train tapping the wheels – he knew by the sound of the tap that all was well.

In winter it was very cold in the carriages – the only heating was from foot warmers. These had some chemical mixture in them which retained the heat. They were an oval, copper cylinder about 50 centimetres long and nearly 20 across and perhaps 15 thick. They were heated before the journey began and as they cooled the passengers shook them to generate more heat.

We had a refreshment stop for a cup of tea and ham sandwich at either Tadmore or Tapawera, then the guard came through the carriages to light the lamps in preparation for a series of tunnels. Although we shut the windows the smoke from the engine usually still got in and it was a relief to open them again and breathe fresh air as we travelled through the tiny settlements of Kiwi, Tui and Rata before reaching the terminus at Glenhope. Here there was a big collection of buildings. As well as the station, there were engine sheds, goods sheds, homes for the workers, stables for Newman's horses and their coaches, and there were also stables for the horses which pulled the big covered wagons that took goods over to Murchison. The most important building for the train passengers was the accommodation house where they were served a hot dinner to prepare them for their coach journey down the Hope River and then through the Buller Gorge.

Before the line was pulled up it had been extended to Kawatiri with the idea that it would eventually go through to Westport to carry coal out of the area. What a scenic tourist trip that would have been! But sadly, it's now just history.

The iron horse

Ian McLaren

'I WOULD LIKE to be an engine driver.' This was probably the response from every second boy in my primary school days when asked about what he'd like to be when he grew up. Very few fulfilled that dream, but my elder brother did – through application and hard work. I was always pleased to visit him at work at the Dunedin station during the 1960s, when he was the driver on the steam express to Invercargill. By the time I got off work the express had already arrived at the station. There always seemed to be great urgency in preparing the engine for the forthcoming journey. My brother, a large oilcan in one hand and a rag in the other, oiled the pistons and other moving parts on both sides of the powerful engine, while the fireman was just as busy, shovelling coal to build up a full head of steam. Both were so proficient at their jobs that they could chat while they worked.

Once I was allowed onto the engine platform to see the engine driver's seat and his view of the track ahead and I saw the fireman's view on the offside of the train, but I found it almost unbearably hot. I was assured it was more pleasant when the train was moving. In the 10 minutes or so that the express was at the station, the engine panted with pent-up power for the journey ahead, amidst loud hissing and clouds of steam. Passengers had disgorged from the six carriages and there seemed to be piles of luggage and freight being unloaded and loaded into the guard's van at the rear. In those days, plenty of people travelled by rail, no doubt in response to the railways slogan: 'Travel in Comfort, Safety and Economy'. Usually two carriages were set aside for first-class travel. On-going passengers refreshed themselves at the station cafeteria with tea – served in those distinctive white cups – thick ham sandwiches or a substantial slab of fruitcake.

All the while a skilled technician would be sounding all the carriage and engine wheels with a steel rod to check that no cracks had developed. When everything was under control my brother and the fireman had their tea from a flask. Often this was their only short break after driving a goods train to Palmerston, about 60 miles north of Dunedin, and then taking over the express train there for its journey south.

It was most important that the express leave right on time at four o'clock. It had to maintain a strict schedule of arrivals and departures on the way. At three minutes to four the stationmaster called out loudly, 'All aboard, please', and then he would repeat the call a number of times.

At one minute to four the station bell was rung as a further warning and two porters closed all the carriage doors. Then, right on four o'clock, the guard blew his whistle from his van and waved a flag to signal to the driver that all was clear and everything set to go. The engine driver waved his arm in acknowledgement, blew the train's whistle and released the brakes with a loud hiss. Almost simultaneously, power was applied and a deep chug would come from the engine. The train moved and, with a brief wave, my brother was on his way. More power, more chugs, more speed, and the guard's van receded into the distance with the smoke flattening out above the train as the speed increased.

I returned to my work marvelling at the smooth, but intense, operation that accompanied the departure of the steam express to Invercargill.

Manapouri holiday in the 1930s

Malvina Middlemiss

DURING THE 1930s my parents and I stayed for the first time at Grand View House, which the Murrell family had established at Lake Manapouri in 1889. In those days dining tables were covered with snow-white, starched linen tablecloths on which sat attractively folded napkins of the same material. A glass jug of water and glasses were always on each table and cutlery was highly polished silverware or silver plate. What a lot of work it all must have been.

On our first evening there, a friend (who was also well-known to the Murrells) came to visit me. We were invited to supper in the kitchen which was a fascinating room – long and narrow. Most of one end was taken up with a black, double-oven, solid fuel-burning range. Down the centre of the room was a long table and on the other side, under the windows, were sinks, workbenches and store cupboards.

In the kitchen I met another member of the household: a big, tame, white cockatoo. In the daytime, he would often perch on the high tree-tops waiting for the returning ferry which he would circle as it drew alongside the jetty. In rough weather and at night he lived in his cage in the kitchen. At suppertime Cocky would join the family for a social hour and chat. He could recite all the parrot phrases perfectly – 'Cocky wants a drink' was his favourite. He liked someone to hold out a spoonful of sweet tea to him and if no one provided it quickly enough the bird would let out a wicked laugh and then reel off a long burst of strong language.

In 1939 I stayed for a few days as a family guest of the Murrells and, between being taken for launch trips, I saw something of the effort required to run a guesthouse. I remember ironing a huge pile of pillowcases and helping to polish trays of cutlery.

Frequently there were overseas tourists at the Grand View and one foggy morning most of the guests stayed in the sitting room rather than experience the peaceful lakeside atmosphere.

'I'll fix them,' the youngest Murrell whispered to me and he tossed an armful of wood on the fire and poured kerosene over the lot. Within minutes the room was so hot everyone decided to head down to the jetty for a launch trip.

A friend of mine was terrified during one trip to the West Arm of Lake Manapouri when a sudden storm broke with rain pelting down and high waves crashing over the launch. The boat had to slow to almost a stop and everyone was cold and wet, but as soon as they arrived at West Arm's one-roomed hut a huge fire was lit and the women were able to get some warmth and dry their clothes. The return trip was gentler but my friend was still so shaken when she reached the guesthouse that Miss Murrell filled her a hot-water bottle and put her to bed. It must have been quite an experience for my friend, as she didn't take up the offer of another trip the next day, which was fine and calm.

On one of my launch trips the skipper went below to switch off the engines so that we could enjoy the silence and asked me to hold the tiller just near where the mountainside rises straight up from the water. One elderly tourist must have had little faith in my ability because he thought we were heading for the cliff-face and grabbed the tiller, which caused the launch to suddenly turn broadside on to the rippling current. The tourist was given a suitable nautical tongue-lashing.

It was mid-winter in 1955 before I got back to Manapouri, and while the place had grown a bit too much for my liking, the warm welcome at Grand View was just the same. Miss Murrell invited me to a cup of tea in the kitchen and then a walk while the sun was still out. I realised how different it was in winter. The ground was frozen hard and, sadly, the tall beech trees near the lakeside now had tins, bottles and other rubbish scattered around under them.

Back in the warm kitchen Miss Murrell was preparing dinner. A knock at the front door announced that a carload of travellers had arrived for a meal and my husband was handed a pumpkin and apples to peel while Miss Murrell began making pastry for a pie. She handed me a saucepan, pointed to custard powder, dried milk and sugar and asked me to do the custard. Luckily, my effort was successful.

We stayed two nights and when my husband went to pay our account he was told that 'visitors' weren't charged. He sought advice from some other guests who were regular weekenders there. 'She is always the same,' they said. 'Just leave your payment on the dressing table.'

It was 1987 before my next visit and another generation of Murrells were running the guesthouse. The welcome was just the same and I'm sure the tradition continues.

A merry Christmas

John Buckland

AT CHRISTMAS TIME I always remember my childhood days when my parents struggled desperately during the Depression to live within their means in a house with no modern conveniences in the bush-clad part of the Inangahua Valley. They always had the worry of finding something suitable for my two sisters and I as presents, but my stocking always had a few fun surprises. Besides a bag of marbles, a rubber ball and some sweets, there was often a lump of coal or a piece of wood wrapped in gaudy paper which helped to make my stocking full, and Dad sometimes made a kite or a wooden toy to keep me happy. My mother's birthday was also on Christmas Day but that didn't ease her workload, as she did her best to cook a special dinner. Mr O'Malley, the local publican and an old family friend, also celebrated his birthday on Christmas Day so they were great birthday cobbers. Mr O'Malley's favourite hobby was keeping a flock of geese, and a few days before Christmas he would arrive with a nice fat gosling for Mother's special birthday dinner. I always had the job of plucking and preparing it for roasting in Mother's small coal range. Feathers flew everywhere as I gathered quills to make potato pop-guns. With Dad's help, the bird was ready for Mum to stuff for the big event next day. On Christmas morning Mr O'Malley arrived with a bottle of wine to celebrate. My mother had one glass, but Dad, Grandfather and Mr O'Malley would finish the bottle in a very happy mood.

A shocking experience

Allan Smith

ABOUT FIFTY YEARS ago I was working on a South Canterbury dairy farm where we used an electric fence to feed out a crop of swedes in 'breaks'. This meant that we had to move the whole fence a few yards each day or so to give the cows fresh fodder.

One day, Hector and I went out to move the fence and I think he must have been in a frivolous mood because he bet me that I couldn't move the fence without walking away up to the far end of the paddock to turn the electric unit off. I told him that if he could do it then I could. We pulled up the fence stakes then spaced ourselves across the fence, which was now lying on the ground, before picking up the wire in our bare hands and walking across the paddock with it to the new position. This meant that every pulsation of the 12-volt shock went through me with a rather uncomfortable belt and a jerk of my whole body!

I was thankful when Hector yelled, 'Far enough', and we both dropped the wire. Before we started re-erecting the fence I asked Hector why he wasn't jerking or feeling the shocks like I was. He told me he had perfectly dry feet and that I must have holes in my gumboots and have wet feet. That was quite true, my feet were damp.

It was, of course, a silly thing to do but we had a laugh or two for many years over this 'electrifying' afternoon experience!

Cavemen of Birdlings Flat

Irene Peddie

MY FATHER WAS always a dedicated fisherman and when he was a young man in the early 1920s he found Birdlings Flat on Banks Peninsula a wonderful place for his obsession. Regardless of the weather, he cycled out there on a Saturday afternoon and returned home late Sunday evening. However, he often found it difficult to anchor his small tent pegs in the shingle, as it always seemed to be windy. On the far side of Lake Forsythe he'd noticed a large cave in the rock halfway up a hill, and the local farmer gave him permission to convert the cave into a campsite. He removed loose rocks with a light blast of dynamite, concreted the floor area, and whitewashed the entire interior. He boarded up part of the entrance, leaving a very narrow door and a window large enough to show the wonderful view. He installed a small pot-bellied stove with a top large enough to take a kettle or saucepan.

From Dad's 'eyrie' we could look out to the end of the lake and then out to sea, while on another side we could see many of the Banks Peninsula hills. This cave served us very well as a cosy, if unusual, holiday retreat, and I remember how quiet and peaceful it was inside even if a storm was raging outside. Our cave was always beautifully cool even on the hottest summer's day and in winter the little stove very quickly warmed the place. At Christmas time Father Christmas even managed to squeeze through the very narrow door!

Access to the cave was by a zigzag track from the edge of the lake and up the grassy slope to the cliff-face. We usually rowed across the lake with our holiday paraphernalia, as it was a long walk around the shingle lakeside.

Our water supply came from a cave nearby where, dripping from the roof, was a spring which never dried up, even in summer. We installed a barrel to catch the water, which was crystal clear although it did have a peculiar taste of milk of magnesia – but we never bothered to boil it before drinking.

Our cave had many nooks, ledges and crannies in the walls, which were very handy as safe places to put a candlestick holder or a cup of tea.

Next to our cave was a shelf of rock that Dad had covered with a smooth coat of concrete and this made a comfortable working bench where we washed ourselves and the dishes, and stored buckets.

One side of the hill went steeply down to the lake to an area we called 'the harbour'. The water was very deep and the sheer rock had no footholds at all, so that if you slipped in, you couldn't scramble out again. I was about four then and was warned never to go near the harbour as the taniwha would snatch me and take me under the water with him forever.

Most of the regular fishermen had fishing stands to enable them to throw their lines further out to sea. These stands were about 10 feet tall and sturdily built, with a solid platform on the top. From the platform Dad whirled the fishing trace, complete with heavy sinker and two or three large baited hooks, round and round his head. At the crucial moment he released the line and the neat coil at his feet quickly unravelled as the trace went well out to sea. Many a good line, plus hooks and sinker, were lost because the end of the line hadn't been tied to the stand before it was launched. The early fisherman got the best catch and it was quite usual to have landed a good groper before lunchtime. Ling, sharks and large red cod were common, too.

When the stand wasn't in use, it was tipped on its side and rolled up the shingle beach until it was above high-water mark and, hopefully, out of reach of a heavy surf. If the sea was too rough for fishing, the men put a net in the lake overnight and this provided enough flounders for a good meal.

Birdlings Flat was a fisherman's utopia and we used our cave as a holiday retreat for some years. But after a strong earthquake the roof leaked so badly after rain that we realised the hill and the cliff had moved so much that it had become unstable. Sadly, our peaceful haven was no longer safe and, reluctantly, we abandoned it.

Later, we had a bach on the other side of the lake but it never had the magic of our cave.

Summer holidays

A Kay Carter

THERE WAS ALWAYS excitement as the time to tow the caravan from the orchard to the front of the house approached. Dad would park it on the oval-shaped gravel drive and there was the aroma of baking filling the air as Mum prepared our favourite cakes, which were stored in tins in the caravan cupboards. Preparations took several days. My brother and I selected favourite games and puzzles, in case there was rain. Dad checked his fishing gear, rummaging through his green canvas bag of sinkers, hooks and flies. He sharpened his big knife and checked the flat steel he used for prising paua or oysters off the rocks. Then he gave the outboard motor a run on a stand with the propeller immersed in a 44-gallon drum of water. All the tools he might need were packed, along with the oars and rowlocks before the dinghy was loaded. He loaded the folding card table and deck chairs, the awning, poles, ropes and tent pegs, outboard motor, anchor, and the meat safe to hang under a shady tree. With the dinghy on top of the car and the caravan behind we looked like a gypsy caravan.

Our plywood caravan was second-hand at best but Dad had remodelled the inside to Mum's specifications, with the table folding into a double bed at night and a single bunk at the towbar end. I slept inside and my brother had his camp stretcher under the awning.

We always asked where we were going and the answer was always the same: 'We'll tell you where we've been when we get back.' We never learned not to ask and it became a family joke. We would sing songs or play games such as 'I spy' and 'See a white horse and make a wish'. The wish would come true if the first dog we saw was black. There was a game with magpies that I can't quite remember, something like one for joy, and two for sorrow, three for a girl and four for a boy. As soon as a squashed possum was sighted we would sing, 'One dead possum lying on the road' to the tune of 'Ten Green Bottles Hanging On the Wall'. When we were older we practised the mental arithmetic of adding up the number-plates of oncoming cars and naming colours, countries, cities and rivers according to the initials on number-plates that came racing towards us.

A favourite saying was, 'This is new territory', as we were told the names of towns and stories of the places we travelled through.

We went after flounder at low tide in the flats of Raglan, Dad carrying a kerosene lantern and a spear. If we moved very slowly and quietly we could make out the shape of a flounder as it lay still on the sandy bottom. Dad would spear it and, still wriggling, it was put in a bucket. Another adventure at Raglan was to cross the inlet, pull the boat up high on the beach, and run in the sand hills. The metal roads presented a challenge and on one trip a stone punctured the petrol tank. While Dad stopped the flow with his finger, the rest of us chewed gum frantically to provide him with a plug.

But most of all, as we grew into our teens, the place we wanted to be was Mount Maunganui. That was where the action was for the younger set and was probably why it was not a favourite spot for our parents. At Christmas and New Year there were beauty competitions for the younger age groups at most of the larger camping grounds. There were concerts and organised games and of course Santa Claus visited with a lolly scramble and plenty of 'ho, ho, ho'.

The sea was fun and Dad made a surfboard for us, heavy compared with the designs of today, but we were proud of it.

There were evangelists who preached to groups of teenagers on the beach and crowds would gather, not so much to listen to their message, but to see who else was at the Mount.

'This is new territory,' I'd say to my own children many years later. 'We'll tell you where we've been when we get back.'

Here is the 'buggy' that Dad and I used to travel in to the sale.

Farming at Cave

Brian Leslie

IN THE 1920s my family moved from a farm in Waikato to one near Cave in South Canterbury. I learned to milk on a tough old cow called May. I couldn't get out of the job even though I hated it, but Dad regarded milking as a rest after plodding after the horse all day. We milked the cows into four-gallon square kerosene tins, but they had to be given a good cleaning before being used for milk. After taking out the house milk, the rest was put through the cream separator while still warm. The separator handle was turned at 60 revolutions a minute to get the correct speed to send the cream out the top spout and the skim milk out the lower spout. Skim milk, along with house food scraps, was fed to the fowls, pigs or dogs. The cream was sold to the butter factory whose lorry came once a week in winter and two or three times a week in summer to collect it. Enough was kept back to make our own butter which was made by putting cream into a butter churn, a circular machine made of white pine or kauri which are woods which don't taint the milk or cream. The churn had an opening in the top with a close-fitting wooden lid and there was a hole right through the centre of each side with a metal centre through which the axle went with a handle on one end. The axle fitted into two beaters which, when the handle was turned, beat the cream, and eventually turned the cream into butter and buttermilk. The buttermilk was let out through a small hole in the bottom, blocked by a cork when the churn was in use, and the butter taken out through the top opening. The butter was then worked with a pair of butter pats made of small pieces of white pine or kauri. The pats were about nine inches long, three inches wide, and about half an inch thick with grooves along one side. These, and the churn, had to be scalded with boiling water, then rinsed in cold, to stop the butter sticking to them before use. When the excess buttermilk was worked out, salt was added and worked into the butter. If it was for sale, it was made into one-pound blocks and wrapped in greaseproof paper. If for home use, it was made into convenient-sized blocks and put into the coolest place available. Dad's mother, who lived in Christchurch, had an artesian well which flowed all the time into an earthenware container about two feet above the ground. She kept the butter in that before the days of refrigerators. On the farm we had no power so we put the butter on a flat, shallow dish, put water in the dish, and a tea towel over it. The water soaked up into the tea towel, evaporated, and so kept the butter cool.

I remember one of my birthdays when we went down to the Te Ngawai River bird-nesting. We would hunt among the gorse bushes and willow for thrushes' and blackbirds' nests and then sell the eggs and heads of the birds. We blew the eggs by pushing a hole in each end and blowing out the contents, but when the egg contained a young bird near to hatching this was difficult. The eggs and heads were sold to the local riding member Mr Smith, who owned Mona Vale farm. The Mackenzie County Council paid a bounty of tuppence per dozen birds' eggs. Some of the boys used to put ink spots on starlings' eggs and call

Swimming pool in the 1930s. The boat is an old washtub in a water hole inhabited by frogs and tadpoles.

them thrushes' eggs. But the starlings' eggs were a lighter colour than the thrushes' eggs and could be told apart. After I'd sold them they were squashed underfoot. Flies were always a problem with the eggs and heads. I used to put Kerol disinfectant among the heads, but that wasn't always satisfactory, even when the heads were strung on wires.

Helping with Christmas dinner in 1946

Neill Todd

AN EARLY START on Christmas morning was essential. Well, that's what I thought as I removed the presents Santa had left in my stocking. As a young lad I was more interested in my presents, but Mum's urging to get breakfast over and to start to help with the preparations for Christmas dinner got me into action. Dad went out into the garden to dig up some new potatoes whilst I was given a basket and told to pick the peas. It was a pleasant task and gave me a chance to do some quality testing. I had to shell the peas and was given an enamel colander, told to sit on the back step and to whistle while shelling. The back steps were below the kitchen window and Mum frequently said she couldn't hear me whistling, though I did my best to keep going.

My next job was to help set the table with the best linen tablecloth and then the cutlery. I was given a clean tea towel and told to carefully wipe the best knives, forks and spoons from the sideboard and then to place them around the table. Wiping the cutlery wasn't so bad but placing it around the table with the proper settings confused me. I was left-handed, which didn't help, but I still managed and later noticed my older sister carrying out adjustments. Our kitchen was compact and the smells of the roast leg of lamb and the other cooking were a strong

Neil Todd's 1946
Christmas mantelpiece.

attraction but I wasn't needed until it was time to stir the gravy. I stirred with great care as burnt gravy meant I was in trouble. Soon uncles, aunties and cousins arrived and the festivities began. Grandma said grace and eating commenced.

After all these years I can still remember the sight and smell of that roast lamb and the new potatoes, peas, beans, cauliflower and pumpkin all fresh from the garden. Then Christmas pudding with its sixpences and threepences, custard, cream, fruit salad, and trifle.

Stout work in Waikato

Ray Neels

TE MIRO IS a small Waikato farming community in the hills about 14 kilometres west of Cambridge. Sometimes it is called Sanatorium Hill because of a tuberculosis hospital which was there in the 1920s. In spring the tuis are loud and excited in the kowhai trees surrounding the ruins of the old hospital but in winter it is often bleak and cold.

One winter, just after the First World War, the area became home to a small group of ex-servicemen and their wives as part of the numerous settlement schemes for soldiers. There was very little, if any, financial assistance given to the new settlers. In that bleak mid-winter around Te Miro it must have been a daunting prospect in almost impossible conditions. For my father and mother, this was their first venture in their married life. My father had had part of his jaw shot away at Gallipoli, so things were extra hard for him. But they made the best of it, as did other settlers. But eventually, all but one family walked off the land with what little possessions they had. In later years they spoke very little about the experience other than in terms of it being rather tragic. However, one story remains in my memory.

To obtain supplies we had to travel by pony and trap down the steep winding track to Cambridge about once a fortnight. The first time my parents went the trap was well loaded, and about halfway back up the pony refused to go any further. My father thereupon opened a bottle of stout they bought as part of their provisions and gave the pony a drink, and he probably had one himself. The ploy worked and they were able to continue the journey home. From then on, the pony always stopped at that point and refused any further co-operation until the magic bottle of stout was produced.

Mother Christmas

Valerie W Smith

FATHER CHRISTMAS AT children's parties or parades is usually a fat, jolly, elderly gentleman, but on at least one memorable occasion he was anything but that. In fact, under his disguise he was a frightened, skinny schoolgirl, press-ganged into filling this role simply because there was nobody else. Late in the Second World War, our local kindergarten was without a Santa for its end-of-year party. The gardener who normally obliged was in hospital, and the nurses wouldn't let him out, even for this great occasion. Every other likely male was either away fighting or hard at work. The milkman and minister were far too busy and the postie was a woman! The head kindy lady was moaning to my mother about this great tragedy just as I arrived home from high school, wilting after the long, hot bike ride. Miss Naylor's face lit up. I would be the perfect Santa because I was tall and always took part in our local plays. Besides, with five little brothers I was used to children making a noise and asking awkward questions. This was my great chance, she told me. My mother was doubtful. 'She's only 14,' she protested weakly. I listened in growing horror as Miss Naylor spoke passionately about the tragedy of a Santa-less Christmas party – the broken hearts, shattered illusions, ruined childhoods, and my tormented conscience if I let this happen. There was even mention of a half-crown tip. My mother gave in. Nobody listened to *my* views.

On the great day, clad in a thick padded suit, enormous boots, whiskers and eyebrows, I shouldered my heavy sack into the kindy kitchen and shuffled into the hall. This entrance was my finest ever. The reception was equal to that of any modern pop star. Instead of shameful exposure and ridicule, I found little faces radiant with excitement and wonder and the room ringing with cries of joy. I'd never experienced such flattering adulation, and, forgetting I was an impostor, I relaxed and threw myself into the Santa role. With the pillow tied to my front, sitting was difficult, as was finding enough room for each child on my lap, but I gave my carefully rehearsed, 'ho, ho, ho', and chuckled benignly. As the hall heated up perspiration stung my eyes, making reading names hard, and my eyebrows and whiskers tickled. The padded costume prickled as sweat ran, but in true patriotic and film star spirit, I bravely carried on till my sack was empty. Then I rose with dignity and difficulty and, to more loud cheers, prepared to leave. As I stepped over a low stool my boot caught in a voluminous trouser leg and I fell backwards. My big black boot flew off and there, for all to see, was a smooth young leg ending in a regulation high school sandal and white sock. The children were too absorbed in the simple gifts and too distraught at seeing beloved Santa on his back to notice much. Except for one boy, someone's older brother, bored and more worldly than the younger children, who cornered me as I shivered with mortification in the kitchen. 'You're not Father Christmas! You're a kid, just like me. Wait till I tell!' We held a whispered discussion on secrecy, honour, being a gentleman, fair play, and finally threats, blackmail and bribery. I offered him sixpence of my hard-earned half-crown, promising to pay it if he kept quiet at least till after Christmas. After that the children would probably have forgotten and, with luck, he also may have forgotten – or been abducted by aliens! As for me, I wouldn't be there to writhe in embarrassment. I'd be on a big ship, on my way to Hollywood. Despite the disastrous finale, I had tasted the bright footlights. Though my joy in theatre was destined to be on the other side of those lights, I was, in those first astonished moments as the kindy Santa, a star!

My first car

Noel Fraser

IN 1946, AT the age of 18, I owned a 1926 Chevrolet tourer. It was my first car and I used it to scoot around our farming and fruit-growing district of Havelock North. After a hot day fruit-picking, my mate Ron and I often went for a swim in the Tukituki River, 10 miles away. One hot Saturday evening, we went to Ocean Beach about 10 miles further on. The last couple of miles were through private land, then down a steep, narrow cliff track to the beach. We had our swim and then, just after dark, got back into the car to head home. We had just started up the cliff track when the car lights went out, leaving us stranded in pitch darkness. We backed cautiously down onto the flat again and went over to the only bach we could see to try and borrow a torch. But the best they could provide us with was a candle! Luckily, there was no wind.

After poking about and changing fuses we discovered that the dash light was the only one that would work. We disconnected the wire from that light and, with an extra piece of wire that we found under the front seat, we extended it. Now it reached the side of the windscreen and gave us just enough light on the left side of the car for us to see where we were going. Cautiously, we drove up the cliff again, along the farm track, and out onto the road. When we got to the tarseal we found it harder to see where we were going because it was so much darker than

At the Turangakumu summit on the Napier-Taupo road in 1946.

the light gravel. We ran off the road onto the grass a few times and then, eventually, our makeshift light failed totally and we were resigned to sitting on the side of the road until daylight. But a car came along and stopped. It was a farming family who had been to the pictures in Hastings and they offered to tow us to the top of Limeworks Hill, which was about a mile away. There, they cast us adrift and then followed us down to light the way. We were within 100 yards of the bottom of the hill when our feeble light came on again. We didn't dare stop until we got home!

Christmas in the early thirties

Joan Snow

TIMES BECAME HARD in the Depression and Dad had to sell his fledgling carrier business as well as our house, but he hung onto his Chev car. We moved into a humble little place near Featherston but our parents made Christmas exciting. There was the suffocating anticipation of Christmas Eve. We'd hang a pillowcase over a chair by our beds and although we vowed we'd simply never go to sleep we must have, because in next to no time it was dawn and there was a lumpy pillowcase. The little odds and ends in it delighted us. However, more was to come. Once we were up and dressed we all lent a hand to load up the car for a week's camping out at the wild and free Palliser Bay. The carrier was loaded with sacks and boxes while the running board and the space between the front mudguards and the motor were packed up high. Then, with each of us clutching our favourite gift, we climbed aboard and we were off, we four kids sitting in the back. The side curtains were taken off and the warm summer air wafted around us. We sang lustily and there was keen competition over who would be the first to glimpse the sea. We wound down the steep Huripi hill and out onto the rutted tracks along the coast. It was lovely, with the sound of cicadas, the hush and curl of the waves on the smooth clean sand, and the smell of creosote on the tents. In no time the canvas was down on

the tent floor, the mattresses lugged in and the beds made up. Then we had the campfire lit, the black billy hung over it on number-eight wire hooks, and we enjoyed the first of many delicious simple meals.

While we explored the beach, climbed the hills and dabbled in rock pools, Dad got out his fishing gear and baited the three hooks. He usually used rabbit meat if he'd been lucky enough to come across a dead one on the road. He didn't have a rod for fishing off the beach, but used a stout green line, which he could throw out and over the breakers with great expertise. If the sea was calm, we always caught fish, but if a dreaded blind eel was hooked then that was the end of fishing for that day. Their slime and smell drove the fish away.

As the sun went down over the distant Kaikouras we all drifted, sunburnt and sleepy, back to camp. With dusk falling we'd gladly snuggle into our beds, and listen to the sea's lullaby, the quiet drone of sleepy cicadas and savour the salty smell of the sea and the smoke from the driftwood fire. So we slept in utter contentment and security to awake all renewed for another gorgeous summer's day.

My flag gaffe

Vic Vaughan

IT WAS 1936 and I was a young post office employee stationed at
Ormondville, a small country town in southern Hawke's Bay. King
George V died on 20 January and it is the custom on the death of a
ruling monarch that flags flown on government buildings throughout
the country are lowered to half-mast and stay at half-mast until the
proclamation of the new monarch. In Ormondville, the 1936 ceremony
of proclaiming the new king took the form of a public function held in
front of the post office, the only government building in the town flying
a flag. The chairman of the town board officiated and at a specific point
in the ceremony the flag was to be lowered from half-mast to ground
level, held there until the actual proclamation of the new king was read,
and then hoisted to the mast-head.

I had been given the task of looking after the flag during the
ceremony and I dutifully performed on cue until the closing stages. I
had only just begun the final hoisting of the flag when a local clergyman
stepped forward, tapped me on the shoulder and pointed out that I had
the flag upside down. Hastily, and somewhat shamefacedly, I had to
rectify the situation and quickly get the flag up the mast the right way
up!

I worked out that when I had lowered the flag, and while listening
intently for my cue to raise it, I had inadvertently allowed the flag and

halyard to pass through my hands, leaving the flag inverted when I began to raise it. That a clergyman put me right may well be an example of divine intervention!

Newspaper delivery

Florence Salisbury

MY SISTER AND I were not really desperate for pocket money but we decided we'd like a regular supply of funds, so when we saw a notice in the local newsagent's window for paper delivery boys for the *Otago Daily Times* we decided we'd give it a try. We had known Mr King the newsagent for years and we knew our district, so we applied. He wasn't sure. He had never heard of girls doing a paper run before, but after he'd checked with our mother, he decided to employ us. We were 12 and 14 and couldn't see what the fuss was all about! Mr King started us on the longest route. He gave us a list of streets and the house numbers and told us to pick up the papers at six in the morning at the taxi depot in Roslyn. We lived on the hill across the valley, so it meant getting out of bed at five, walking up the hill in the dark, counting the papers, and then trudging off. We were supplied with bags that slung over our shoulders and each paper had to be folded and then thrown from the gate onto the front doorstep. We got quite expert at it, always remembering that throwing the paper onto the roof of a house that was below road level was a no-no!

We walked the length of Kaikorai Valley Road and delivered to side-streets as well, so we soon had our own system going to cut down the walking we each had to do. We took alternate streets but always waited for one another at the end. For six months, rain or shine, we walked the route and earned five shillings a week.

One morning, I waited a long time for my sister at the end of one street and was getting anxious. Soon she arrived, out of breath and gasping, 'I fell over a cow.' She regularly delivered to a farm and she hadn't seen the cow sitting right by the gate until it was too late.

If we were lucky we could catch the mill bus back up the valley road because the morning shift at the Roslyn mills started just as we finished our route.

An elderly couple whose house was close to the road asked Mr King to tell us that the paper thudding on their porch disturbed them in the morning, so could we please open the gate, walk up their path and place it on the porch. After that, at 6.30 each morning we placed a neatly folded paper on their doormat and closed the gate quietly so the latch didn't click loudly. Another house had a high wooden fence and a high gate, which was always closed. It was quite an effort to throw the paper over and it was pleasing to hear it drop neatly on the other side. What we didn't know at first was that there was a hole in the drive on the other side and the paper nearly always got wet – a constant source of complaint. After we found out, the plunk as it landed in the puddle became especially satisfying!

One Saturday, when we collected our pay, Mr King told us he'd like to change our route. He'd given us the valley one to test us and we'd passed with flying colours. We got a hill route next and it was a doddle after the last one and we really enjoyed it. One of our customers told Mr King that he could set his alarm by us and, in fact, if we heard his alarm clock ring as we reached his gate in the morning we knew we were up to time. The man asked Mr King why hadn't he had girls on the run before? In his opinion they were much more reliable.

At Christmas, the agent gave us a card and we knocked on the customers' doors and politely said who we were. If the householder was in a generous mood we got a good Christmas box. The man with the alarm clock gave us a whole shilling! When we'd counted all the threepences, sixpences and the occasional shilling there was the princely sum of £10. We really felt rich.

I treated my sister to a night at the opera *Carmen*, at which stall seats were seven and sixpence. What a Christmas we had that year. We feel we struck a blow for feminism long before it became fashionable.

New Year's Eve oats

Jean Smith

WHEN WE WERE young, bedtime came early and seldom extended to seeing in the New Year, but one holiday our family and others pooled resources to buy some fireworks which included a basket-bomb, made up of explosives in a straw package about the size of a building block.

First came the sparklers, crackers and Catherine wheels, with the basket-bomb kept for the climax. It was placed in a large kerosene tin, the type often used as coal buckets in those days. Adults and children were herded to the safety of the wide veranda and my father set about lighting the fuse, which extended from the tin. Then he ran for the veranda too. There was a huge bang that reverberated round the Sumner Hills and the tin flew into the air, then landed, bashed beyond recognition. There were screams of excitement or terror, according to age. Those bombs were probably imported from China, but they were highly dangerous and must have been banned shortly afterwards, because I never saw another one.

There were other New Year's Eves when we awaited the first caller or first-footer, preferably a dark-haired male, carrying a lump of coal to bring good luck. Relatives had gathered at the Kaka Point family crib and the children, all babies or toddlers, had been put to bed many hours earlier. We five adults sat round the huge wooden table playing some of those games that were popular holiday pastimes or just chatting. I was a nursing mother and I decided I was ravenous, not for any normal party

Jean (right).

fare, but for a very large plate of Fleming's porridge. The others were alpine people used to simple sustaining fare when they were climbing and they were all fans of Sergeant Dan of Creamota fame. What could be more appealing than a large helping of porridge? A Scotsman would have approved and would probably have recommended an accompanying dram of whisky. Quite a New Year feast, porridge and whisky!

The standard-six picnic

Coral Ridling

IT WAS ALMOST the last day of term. The last term of the year and the end of primary school. We were leaving standard six and were already enrolled for the secondary school years ahead. The headmaster had decided to take us for a picnic. We were to travel to Milford Beach by tram, boat and bus, spend the day in the wonderful new swimming pool, and play on the beach. Then we could explore the Pirate Shippe, an exciting replica on which afternoon teas were served every day and which became a popular cabaret and dance floor by night. It seemed to me that the headmaster was rather sweet on my mother, then a youngish widow with dark curly hair and a vivacious personality. She was to accompany us as mother chaperone. The day arrived. The sun shone, the air was light, the water warm, our home-made lunches tasted delicious and we were really enjoying ourselves. The war in Europe and the Middle East seemed a long way away.

At about three o'clock my mother and the headmaster departed for afternoon tea while we frolicked on the beach, licking our ice creams. An hour later they returned, their faces grave. They gathered us around and told us the news they'd just heard on the wireless. The Japanese had bombed Pearl Harbour and America was now at war with Japan. 7 December 1941 – the day of our standard-six picnic.

Bush camp election

Ken Gregory

IN 1943 I was teaching at Te Rena, a bush camp in the King Country. It was an election year and during the evening meal in the cookhouse the main topic of conversation was politics. The men were rabid supporters of Frank Langstone the sitting Labour member. As for the Tories and the 'bosses', what the men said about them was totally unprintable.

One day, I received a large official-looking envelope stamped 'On His Majesty's Service'. It notified me that the Te Rena cookhouse would be an official polling booth and I was to state by return mail whether or not I was prepared to act as deputy returning officer. My chest swelled with pride. Of course I would. I would be assisting the cause of democracy, and getting paid for it. It was rumoured that Frank Langstone was coming because he wanted to meet the boys, the most loyal supporters he had. What an evening that was. The dining room was packed and an enormous fire blazed so that the room was soon stiflingly hot. Far more kerosene lamps than usual lit the room. Bill the bush boss who presided had some difficulty in getting Frank to the front of the room because so many men crowded round wanting to shake his hand. After Bill's speech of welcome, which was punctuated by stamping of feet and whistles of approval, the great man took the floor. His speech was a masterpiece of political invective directed at the

National Party Tories. Every time they were mentioned, a great chorus of boos sent the flames in the lamps trembling, but the noise was nothing compared with the whistles, cheers and stamping which erupted every time the Labour Party was mentioned. Frank played on his audience like the old-time political campaigner that he was. I clapped and stamped with the best of them.

In his speech of thanks, the bush boss said, 'Frank, I can promise you that when the results from this polling booth are posted up, every vote will be for Frank Langstone.'

On polling day I ran a very tight ship and had appointed Dave at the cookhouse to be my poll clerk. I checked to see that the number of voting papers and ballot papers and forms tallied with the official list. There were flimsy wooden screens to make voting booths.

The election was on a Saturday, which was normally a working day for the bushmen but, because it was a polling day, it was to be a holiday. The evening before, the little timber-hauling train made a special trip bringing dozens of five-gallon kegs of beer. They were carried in triumph up to the single men's huts and the party began straight away.

On election morning, at nine o'clock sharp, I proudly threw open the cookhouse door and made sure that the polling booth sign outside was clearly visible. For two hours nothing happened. Dave and I voted and then Bluey wandered in. He was thin and wiry with rather aesthetic features crowned by silver, naturally curly hair. He kept very much to himself, for the very good reason that the others wouldn't talk to him. 'Scabbed on the Queensland wharves in 1918. You don't talk to scum like that.' Bluey voted and then wandered off. The bush boss and his wife voted. The afternoon wore on. Dave produced a pack of cards, and when I wouldn't play poker with him, he played solitaire while I read a book. It began to get dark and was getting close to closing time. 'I'll go and give the men the hurry up,' said Dave.

'I'm closing the poll sharp at seven,' I announced firmly. 'If they're not here, then too bad. They miss out.' Dave looked at me quizzically, 'You tired of life or something?'

As he left he glanced up at the wall clock whose hands were approaching seven. 'That clock is fast by my watch,' he said and moved the hands back quarter of an hour.

Sounds of singing, catcalls, and yahooing could be heard getting closer. Right on the tick of seven, by the clock, the men all stumbled in. Immediately all was chaos, because everybody wanted to vote at once. Hospitably, they offered me a beer, lots and lots of beer, and they were somewhat put out when I refused. I explained that I was on official duty. Tony, wanting to be helpful, suggested that because he was the only sober one I should give him all the voting papers and he would fill them in for everyone. Billy, in a very loud voice, began to tell the world exactly what he thought of Mr Bowles, the National Party candidate who was opposing Mr Langstone. I drew Billy's attention to the sign saying that voters must not discuss politics in this polling place. Billy, who was considered to be a bit of a wit, said that he was not *dis*-cussing that blankety blank Bowles, he was just cussing him. Dave put an end to the nonsense by telling them that if they didn't watch it, their votes wouldn't be counted and then Frank wouldn't be too pleased would he? That sobered them up a bit. Finally, everyone had voted and Dave and I took the ballot box into the kitchen and began the count.

Towards the end of the count, to my utter horror, I opened up one paper – it was the only one which voted for Bowles. Dave looked at me pityingly. 'Gawd,' he said. 'You're for it. You silly bugger. Whatever made you do it?'

'It wasn't me. I swear it,' I bleated. 'Tell that to the jokers out there,' said Dave grimly.

We turned our attention to the licensing poll. The pile of votes for Continuance grew higher and higher and then, utterly aghast, I opened a paper marked Prohibition. Looking sorrowfully at me Dave said slowly, 'Oh dear, dear, dear! You're for it, twice over. We'll finish up here and then, instead of you doing it, I'll post the results up on the cookhouse door. You duck out the back door and tear off down to the tram. I'll delay things as long as I can.'

Not needing any urging, I slipped out the door and ran off into the darkness. I reached my hut and, to my amazement and relief, I found the bush boss and his wife sitting on the bed. 'I hope you don't mind . . .' Bill said. 'But our wireless battery went flat, so we came over to listen to the results on your set.' I just had time to stammer out my troubles when we heard the sounds of shouting and commotion getting nearer. Then there was a great hammering on the hut door. 'Leave this to me,' said Bill quietly, and he opened the door. He held up his hand for silence. 'You've got the wrong one,' he said. 'I happen to know that he voted the right way.'

'Well who did it? Who was it?' voices called. Then someone yelled, 'I know. It was Bluey! It was that old bastard Bluey!' So off they went looking for Bluey, but he'd gone fishing.

Bluey was a queer old bloke. Some said he even read poetry.

The captain's chicken

Opo

DURING THE LATTER part of 1941 I was doing weekend duty as officer of the day on HMNZS *Monowai*, a merchant ship converted into an armed merchant cruiser, which was berthed at the naval base in Auckland. A petty officer cook, who was the cook for the captain, asked to see me. He was jabbering away incoherently and all I could understand was, 'The captain's chicken, sir . . .' Eventually I got the story from him. He had been cooking a meal for the captain's dinner party that evening and had taken the roast chicken out of the galley oven and set it on top of the stove while he checked the progress of the roast vegetables. When he turned to baste the chicken a moment later, it had completely disappeared!

I was only a sub-lieutenant then with little experience, so I sent for the experienced master-at-arms and told him the story. When I asked if I should have the ship searched he roared with laughter and said, 'You can have the ship searched from trunk to keel if you like, sir, but you won't find a feather!'

I left the hapless cook to sort out his problem and promptly forgot about the incident until about 15 years later. I was back in 'civvy street' and happened to be honorary secretary of the Gisborne Yacht Club. I joined the other club members on a social visit to Tuai where we enjoyed some not-too-serious competitive sailing against the Tuai Yacht

Club on the hydro lake near the village. We were billeted with club members for the weekend and I had enjoyed a couple of beers and a splendid meal with my host family when my host said, 'You were on the *Monowai*, weren't you?' I told him that I had been on her for the whole commission.

'Remember me?' he said. I had to confess I didn't. 'Do you remember the captain's chicken that disappeared?'

'Vividly,' I said.

'Well . . .' he said. 'I was the culprit!' Then facts emerged. He had been the duty stoker that day and part of his duty was to check and record the temperature of the galley freezers every two hours. On his way to the freezer chamber he had passed through the captain's galley and seen the freshly cooked chicken sizzling in its pan on the top of the stove. Noticing that the cook was preoccupied, he whisked the bird out of its pan and into his boiler suit and without even breaking his step he continued on into the freezer chamber. There, concealed behind the door, he'd eaten it! He confessed he hadn't enjoyed it too much. The chicken was too hot to be eaten quickly and after a few moments the cold of the freezer had made him start to shiver, but he was under pressure to eat the bird and dispose of the carcass before he was interrupted.

At least his belated confession solved the mystery that had puzzled me all those years, but I never did discover what the captain's guests ate for dinner that evening.

The Devil's Elbow

Marjorie Henderson

IN THE EARLY 1920s we lived in Napier. One Sunday, our parents took the family for a picnic to Lake Tutira, on the Napier to Wairoa road. We had a big open-top Buick, which comfortably held Mum, Dad and five children. After the picnic my father, who enjoyed a good adventure, decided to drive home by a secondary road, which took us over a wild, winding and spectacular route along the side of a steep ridge overhanging a deep valley. I think it was called the Devil's Elbow Road. All went well for a while but then the road started to get worse. Bits of bank had fallen onto the road and the edges had fallen into the valley. Suddenly, we came to a huge, deep hole in the middle of the road. We all piled out while Dad straddled the wheels of the car on each side of the hole, with a boy on each side to direct him. After that the road improved for a while. We thought we were through the worst of it when we came around a corner and there was just no road at all! It had fallen entirely into the valley.

We had no choice but to turn the car round on that narrow road and drive back the way we'd come. Dad must have known how Mum was feeling, so he asked her to walk my little sister and me back along the road while he and the boys backed the car up till they found a possible turning place. To me it was all a tremendous adventure. I even suggested to Mum that it would be exciting if we found that the road had fallen away behind us as well, perhaps where the big hole had been! My poor mother must have been absolutely terrified, miles from anywhere, with two small girls, wondering when she'd see her husband and sons again. However, at long last they came back and picked us up, and we all got home safely, but we never again travelled over the Devil's Elbow Road!

The parade

Allan Smith

MANY YEARS AGO I was in the 1st Canterbury Regiment with the exalted rank of sergeant and I had been ordered to attend a 'beating the retreat' ceremony in Latimer Square one Sunday afternoon. I had even been appointed colour sergeant for the day. Everything was very formal. The regimental band paraded in dress uniform and the regimental officers and their ladies, from the brigadier down, and various civic dignitaries including the mayor were in attendance. Lesser mortals were lined around the perimeter of the square watching while the band played before the flag-raising ceremony. At the appointed moment I marched out to the foot of the flagpole, stood to attention, and began to fix the flag to the halyard. To achieve this, two wooden toggles were hooked onto the flag through two loops on the halyard itself. This simple movement was as easy as doing up the buttons on a coat, but not this time. There was only one toggle on the flag! What on earth was I to do? The band was playing on and the dignitaries were all standing watching me – the officers stiffly at attention. I couldn't hoist the flag with only one toggle because it was the bottom one which would have turned the flag upside down and made it a distress signal! Mind you, I actually was 'in distress'.

However, all was not lost. While the bandmaster squeezed a few

With a knot firmly tied, the flag is raised at last!

extra bars out of his tune and the officers slowly got cramp in their saluting arms, I battled the halyard and tied the flag onto it with a good knot. You could almost hear the sighs of relief when I finally raised the flag to the mast-head. The band completed their number and the officers relaxed. The rest of the formalities have faded from memory, but the comments of various khaki-clad figures who came at me in descending order of seniority are still very clear in my memory. All demanded an explanation of my apparent ineptitude but they were pacified by my explanation that the fault lay with the unit out at Burnham, which had supplied both the flag and the flagpole. They had neglected to check that all was in order before delivery. I must have been forgiven because they still spoke to me and I wasn't reduced in rank or tied to a gun wheel. It couldn't have looked too bad to the general public because a picture of me raising the flag appeared, without comment, in *The Press* the following day.

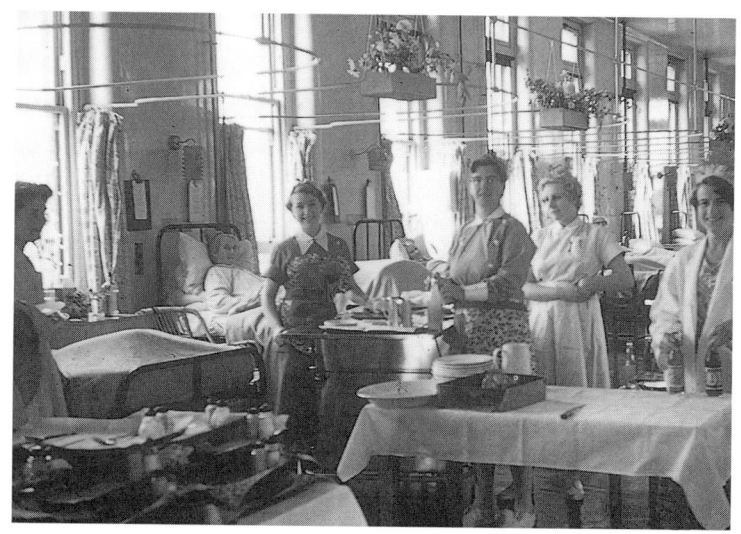

Christmas day on the ward, about 1970.

Two hospitals at Christmas time

Heidi Wassner

I ARRIVED IN New Zealand in October 1953 and was posted immediately to Wellington Hospital. I had been on night duty in the maternity ward and, with other night nurses, went to the supervisor's office at seven on Christmas morning to get a taxi chit for the ride to Kilbirnie. There we all heard of the Tangiwai disaster. At the nurses' home I joined others to listen to the eight o'clock news and went to bed, thinking of the grief and despair of so many families throughout the country. Late in the afternoon, Christmas dinner was served and I was shaken by the contrast between this event and any I had experienced previously. It was summer, the longest day had just passed instead of the short, dull and cold winter days of the northern hemisphere. The table was decorated with paper chains and crackers, and we all wore paper hats. The atmosphere was one of camaraderie and good cheer with no hint of the tragedy of less than 24 hours ago.

By 1961 I was ward sister of a surgical ward in Dunedin Hospital. It was the old, open-plan style with 12 beds down each side and a large table in the middle. On Christmas Eve all available pairs of hands had decorated the ward. Crêpe paper chains were no longer allowed because they were a fire hazard, so we used flowers in every conceivable container and on every visible ledge. Dunedin gardeners brought whatever was colourful from their gardens – lilies, roses, delphiniums, daisies and greenery, and deposited them in tubs in the hospital foyer. Ward staff could come and help themselves and select what was suitable for their designs. Wards vied with each other as to which would look the most decorative. On Christmas morning, day staff came early and night staff stayed longer so that by 10 o'clock all the patients were sponged, beds made, and dressings and treatments completed. This encouraged a festive mood to develop during the next two hours. The matron and medical superintendent, doctors with their families, and nurses from other wards all visited. A member of the hospital board made the round of all wards to distribute the Richmond shilling, the gift of a charitable trust, set up by a North Dunedin publican early in the century. Outside the hospital, the Salvation Army band played Christmas carols and many eyes filled with tears.

Around midday, a dietician brought in a large Christmas cake, carrying it with great dignity around the ward before placing it on the centre table. One of the senior surgeons carved the roast and some junior doctors helped me to serve the vegetables while nurses took the trays to each patient. The whole morning had felt like a family affair, but most patients were grateful for the after-dinner quiet period which finished at two o'clock as the doors swung open to let in the visitors.

I left the ward at four o'clock, tired but totally in harmony with the tradition of a summer Christmas.

Trials of a young teacher

David Rich

IN 1955 I was appointed to my first teaching position at Beckenham School, Christchurch. The large school was under the firm hand of Jimmy Southward whose philosophy of hard work and respect for authority and one's elders was instilled in the pupils at an early age. My classroom's visual aids consisted of a couple of roller maps – one of New Zealand and the other of the world – blackboards and chalk, and a few books on loan from the library service. The wooden-floored, austere classroom had heavy, dual, ink-stained desks, and high windows were set into one of the plastered walls. There was a nature table with a collection of small animals, which had a habit of deserting their boxes and jars and making their homes in other parts of the room. This table was looked upon with some scepticism by the headmaster who considered it rather revolutionary.

This was my probationary assistant's year so I had only 30 pupils in my standard four class. The experienced teachers in the adjoining rooms had upwards of 40. The head had hand-picked my group who were a bright lot and, on the whole, keen to do their best academically. I was young, enthusiastic and innovative in those days. I decided that during the August holidays I would take the class on a field trip to the West Coast for a week. There was no question of the excursion being made in school time. This was considered a holiday rather than a learning

My Standard 4 class wishing me a 'Happy Birthday' on the occasion of my 21st. (Published *Star-Sun* newspaper.)

experience by the Canterbury Education Board, the school committee and especially by the headmaster. Arrangements were made for us to travel by train to Greymouth where we'd be accommodated at the local high school in their manual training wing. We slept on the floors of the home science and woodworking rooms and catered for ourselves using their cooking facilities. During our stay we travelled to local sawmills and coal-mines where we saw huge rimu logs being turned into building timber by the shiny, sap-dripping, double circular saws. We were introduced to some of the last of the pit ponies, hauling the coal trucks far underground.

The most memorable part of the trip, however, wasn't the screech of saws cutting through timber, or the carbide lamps on our miners' helmets at the coal-face, but our brief stop at Arthur's Pass to change engines. The 10-year-old kids were very excited and all disembarked onto the platform while the steam locomotive was exchanged for the electric unit, which would haul us through the tunnel. We gave strict instructions that no pupils were to leave the station as we didn't know how long the operation would take. Before long the exchange was completed, a bell rang, the guard waved a green flag, and we started off. However, two of the boys had visited a shop some distance away as their pocket money was itching to be spent. I was horrified to see the two lads running along and trying to board the carriage. We were fast picking up speed and I immediately pulled the emergency stop lever. It was above a notice threatening a £25 fine for 'improper use'. That was about a month's salary!

With screeching wheels the train came to a stop and the two latecomers clambered aboard. An irate guard appeared, demanding to know who was responsible for pulling the emergency lever. I owned up and was given a very uncomplimentary opinion of what he thought of me. His parting shot threatened dire consequences when he reported me to the Greymouth stationmaster and this had me really worried.

Apparently, the braking system of the carriages wasn't synchronised with that of the electric unit and when the carriages stopped and the locomotive kept going this caused straining and damaging of vital couplings and I was solely responsible for this abuse of railway property. I was heartened by the support of the mother of one of the lads but I awaited the wrath of the stationmaster with trepidation. As it turned out, he was very understanding. He asked me if there'd been a danger of the boys falling beneath the wheels, or of being injured attempting to board the carriage, and when I answered in the affirmative, he told me I'd done the right thing.

Even so, I'd think twice before I ever activated an emergency stop lever again.